SUPPORTING CHILDREN WITH AUTISM IN THE PRIMARY CLASSROOM

This invaluable resource offers a wealth of strategies enabling you to support children with autism in the mainstream classroom. Cutting through the jargon and recognising the huge variety of ways in which children's perceptions, feelings and behaviours may be affected by autism, the text is packed with practical advice to help you to create a classroom environment which will meet the needs of the individual child.

Each chapter of the book addresses some of the most common social, practical and behavioural difficulties that a child with autism may face at school, and details tried and tested approaches for improving their experiences and outcomes in your classroom. Topics discussed include:

- classroom layout, timetables and rules

- effective communication

- supporting learning and setting targets

- breaks, unstructured times and school trips

- challenging behaviours.

Supporting Children with Autism in the Primary Classroom – A Practical Approach is a highly accessible resource which will give primary teachers, teaching assistants, SENCOs and parents, the confidence and knowledge they need to support young children with autism.

Dawn Connor currently works as an Early Years Specialist Support Teacher in Scotland. She is a qualified Primary School Teacher with over twenty years' experience. Dawn currently advises and works with staff in Early Years Establishments to support young children with Additional Support Needs.

SUPPORTING CHILDREN WITH AUTISM IN THE PRIMARY CLASSROOM

A PRACTICAL APPROACH

Dawn Connor

Routledge
Taylor & Francis Group

LONDON AND NEW YORK

First published 2019
by Routledge
2 Park Square, Milton Park, Abingdon, Oxon OX14 4RN

and by Routledge
711 Third Avenue, New York, NY 10017

Routledge is an imprint of the Taylor & Francis Group, an informa business

British Library Cataloguing-in-Publication Data
A catalogue record for this book is available from the British Library

Library of Congress Cataloging-in-Publication Data
Names: Connor, Dawn, 1964- author.
Title: Supporting children with autism in the primary classroom : a practical approach / Dawn Connor.
Description: Milton Park, Abingdon, Oxon ; New York, NY : Routledge, [2018] | Includes bibliographical references and index.
Identifiers: LCCN 2018019852 (print) | LCCN 2018031073 (ebook) | ISBN 9780203712580 (eb) | ISBN 9781138559509 (pbk.) | ISBN 9780203712580 (ebk.)
Subjects: LCSH: Autistic children—Education (Primary) | Autistic children—Education—Curricula.
Classification: LCC LC4717 (ebook) | LCC LC4717 .C66 2018 (print) | DDC 371.94—dc23
LC record available at https://lccn.loc.gov/2018019852

ISBN: 978-1-138-55950-9 (pbk)
ISBN: 978-0-203-71258-0 (ebk)

Typeset in DIN Pro
by Apex CoVantage, LLC

I wish to thank the following people without whose support this book would not have been written: my husband Joe, who has always been there for me, my mum Jeannette, who has been *my* greatest teacher, my late stepdad David, who always had wonderful ideas, my children Barry and Nikki, who never fail to make me proud, my grandchildren Chase, Ace, Brodie and Orla, who light up my world, and my sisters Lesley and Susan who have also been so supportive of me.

Finally, this book is also dedicated to the many children with autism whom I have taught, and their parents. The challenges that they face, on a daily basis, should be an inspiration to all of us.

CONTENTS

ABOUT THE AUTHOR

Dawn Connor is a qualified Primary School Teacher with more than twenty years' experience, who lives and works in Scotland. She has a Master's Degree in Special Education - Autism (Children) from the University of Birmingham.

Dawn currently advises and works with staff in Early Years Establishments to support young children with Additional Support Needs.

Dawn lives in the suburbs of Glasgow, and has a husband, two children and four grandchildren. She enjoys spending time gardening and playing with her grandchildren.

NOTES

For ease of use, I shall be using the following terminology throughout this book: 'child with autism' will be used to refer to a child who has a diagnosis of an Autism Spectrum Condition/Disorder. 'Wee Johnny' will also be used to refer to a child with autism.

There is currently some debate around whether to refer to people who have autism as being 'autistic'. I have chosen to use the terminology 'with autism', as I feel that it describes the condition, without defining the person, and I hope that this does not cause offence to anyone with autism.

'Parents' will be used to refer to any significant caregiver who has responsibility for the child.

INTRODUCTION

This book aims to offer a wealth of strategies to enable you to support children with autism in your mainstream classroom. It is not intended to replace any training on autism that you may wish to undertake, but it will hopefully give you some practical suggestions and advice.

First, let me tell you a little bit about me. I trained and qualified as a primary school teacher in Scotland over twenty years ago, and in my current role as a specialist support teacher, I work with young children who present with a variety of additional support needs, including autism.

I have a Master's Degree in Special Education – Autism (Children) from the University of Birmingham.

I have, in my previous roles, taught within mainstream schools and in two autism bases. Working within these supported bases gave me a real insight into the challenges that children with autism face on a daily basis. Within these specialist classrooms, however, there is usually a higher staff to pupil ratio; this may not be the case in mainstream classrooms, where there is generally one teacher and, perhaps, a classroom assistant.

Throughout my teaching career, I have helped many pupils with autism, and staff, to overcome many of the difficulties that they have faced. Recently, I helped a young boy who was finding school life a bit difficult. I met with his class teacher and suggested strategies that I had previously used to good effect. After my involvement, his teacher commented on how the strategies and advice that I had given to her had made all the difference in making school life a much more positive experience for him, his peers in class and for staff. She suggested that I should put all of my ideas and advice into a book – and so here it is!

Each chapter within the book should reflect some of the most common difficulties that a child with autism may face and will detail some tried and tested approaches that I have successfully used over the years.

At the end of some of the chapters, you will find some helpful suggestions for further reading, should you require this.

Chapter one
AUTISM - WHAT IT CAN 'LOOK LIKE' IN CLASS

Before I begin, I would like to make some important points. Firstly, autism is *not* bad behaviour, a mental health illness, nor is it as a result of poor parenting (Canavan 2016). Autism is a biological disorder that affects how the brain develops, meaning that the autistic brain is developing differently to that of a 'neuro-typical' brain (Shelton & Jalongo 2016). There are four main areas of difficulty for a child with autism (Scottish Intercollegiate Guidelines Network 2017):

- Social communication and interactions

- Restrictive and repetitive behaviours

- The use of imagination and play

- Sensory sensitivities

More about how this is diagnosed, and the specific criteria necessary to meet the requirements of an Autism Spectrum Disorder diagnosis, can be found at the end of this chapter.

Most children with autism I have taught over the years have been male; it is more common for autism to be recognised in boys than in girls (Scottish Intercollegiate Guidelines Network 2017).

In essence, children with autism can think and behave differently to their mainstream peers, and this can therefore pose some challenges for them, and for those who support them. It would help you, I suspect, if I simply listed some of the common

Autism - what it can 'look like' in class

behaviours that I have witnessed over the years in children with autism, and I will begin with some positives.

Children with autism can be:

- Focused and 'driven'
- Honest
- Loyal
- Good at problem solving

They can have:

- Great attention to detail
- Fabulous skills in numeracy or in reading
- A strong awareness of right and wrong
- Good long-term memory recall
- Detailed knowledge about their favourite topics of interest

They may, however, display the following in class:

- Leaving the classroom
- Bouncing up and down on their chair
- Finger flicking or 'waving' their pencil or ruler from side to side
- Walking on tip-toes
- Swiping items off of the desk
- Eating inedible items
- Hiding under the desk or in corners of the room
- Shouting out or screaming

- Difficulties with moving from one piece of work to another

- Not completing work

- Taking too long to complete work

- Self-injurious behaviours, e.g. hitting head, biting hand

- Hitting out at others in class, including staff

- Withdrawn behaviours

- Negative reactions to changes to routines

I have worked with children with autism who have exhibited most of the behaviours mentioned, and so I can appreciate how difficult this can be, especially if you have other children in class who also have difficulties – you may even have more than one child in your class who has autism. This book will hopefully help to explain *why* these behaviours may occur, how best to pre-empt them before they *do*, and some strategies to help you and the child with autism (there is more on this in Chapter 6). This should make life a whole lot easier for the child (or children) with autism in your classroom, and for everyone who supports them.

Girls with autism

Girls with autism can often present very differently to boys. It is important to be aware that even though girls may appear on the surface to be coping, they may be internalising their frustrations at not being understood, or they themselves may not understand what is happening around them, and this may cause problems for them when they go home, resulting sometimes in what is commonly described as a 'meltdown'.

As mentioned earlier, most of the children with autism that I have taught over the years have been boys, but I have also taught a few girls with autism. There are, however, many girls who 'fall under the radar' of diagnosis, and this is usually because they are quite adept at masking their autism by copying the behaviours of their peers in an attempt to 'fit in' with their typically developing female friends (Canavan 2016).

The following may be present in girls with autism in your classroom:

- Anxiety – very often tearful with no obvious (to you) reason

- Sad/depressive behaviours (especially in older girls)

- Copying peers – this is quite unlike most boys who have autism

- Being led by their peers in games, rather than taking the initiative themselves

- Frequently having only one special friend

- 'Disappearing' into fantasy or role-play, taking on the role for themselves

- Demonstrating a lack of eye contact or overly inappropriate eye contact

- Speaking with a higher, or deeper pitched voice

- Having *intense* interests in specific areas – more so than a typically developing peer

You may also see some of the behaviours that were listed earlier – it all depends on the individual girl, their mood at any given time and the environmental factors. More information on girls with autism can be found by accessing the web link at the end of this chapter.

Parents as partners

Let me say something important here; when you have worked with children with autism, you quickly realise that, like their mainstream counterparts, they are all very different, and so what may work for one child, may be wholly inappropriate for another. Therefore, no 'one size fits all' approach will ever work. Similarly, the behaviours mentioned earlier may, or may not, be present in each child who has autism. This is why it is very important to get to know the child, and the best people to give you this information are the parents.

Parents are an invaluable source of information in many areas, and fostering good relationships with them is vital if you want to know more about the child, what makes them 'tick', what upsets them and what motivates them. All of this information is incredibly important in helping you to teach their child in a more meaningful way.

A good way to develop this good working relationship, is to use a home/school diary. Let's be clear, I don't mean a novel – in my experience, parents don't want this either. A jotter cut into two (two diaries for the price of one) would work well. It is good practice to use a home/school diary to communicate key facts about what the child has learned, how they coped that day (or not), whether they ate lunch (if this is an issue) and any other pertinent information, such as upcoming trips or special visitors. It could look like this:

Today Johnny did the following:

- Learned about 'o'clock' times

- Had fish and chips for lunch – ate well

- Found assembly a bit difficult, but remained in the hall

- Homework is his reading book – see homework grid

- Reminder that it is our swimming day tomorrow

A diary should not, however, be a platform for you to complain about what a dreadful time wee Johnny has given *you* today – parents do not *need,* nor *want* to hear this. I know that sometimes you may feel quite stressed, but it is more helpful to parents if you chat to your colleagues about this, the diary is not the place to vent these emotions. Some parents may write in the diary and some may not. Please do not judge a parent if they do not respond. When they *do* respond, it is helpful if a parent can be encouraged to write down how the child is *feeling* that morning, or if they have had a bad evening/night – this can often affect their mood and subsequent learning the next day, but don't be too prescriptive about what a parent should or should not write, as this may put them off writing at all.

Suggested reading

What is autism?: www.autism.org.uk/about/what-is/asd.aspx
Girls and autism: www.autism.org.uk/about/what-is/gender/stories.aspx

Chapter two
THE CLASSROOM ENVIRONMENT

Classroom seating position

So, it's the start of term, you are in your classroom and thinking about where to seat the children. Here are some good points to consider when deciding where to place the child with autism, and some helpful suggestions to support their introduction into your class.

First, let's look at the practicalities in terms of sensory issues. In my experience, it is helpful for a child with autism to be seated with their back to incoming streams of light that can 'blind' them when working. This is a common problem and can often lead to children rising from their chairs to move away from the source of the irritation.

Second, I would avoid seating them in close proximity to the door, as this could be an easy 'escape route' should times become tough for them – we will discuss how the child can best manage these difficult times later, in Chapter 6. I would also add here that it is preferable if the child can face the door – this allows them to see who is coming into the class, and thus prevents any sudden surprises should the door be opened.

Some children with autism can feel 'hemmed in' if sitting closely between two others, and this can often lead to challenging behaviours. I would always position them at the end of a table, with another peer at the opposite end of the table (this will avoid highlighting the child with autism as being 'different').

It is helpful if a child has their photo (or their name, is if this more appropriate) on their chair to denote that it is *their* chair, and it is a good visual cue of where they should be sitting. Similarly, a sample carpet square (available for little cost from carpet stores) is a portable item that can be used to show where they should sit on the carpet – "it's carpet time" or "it's time to sit on the carpet" can be confusing for a child with autism, as the carpet is *everywhere* in the classroom, so exactly *where* should they sit? This can, in itself, cause great anxiety, and this may result in unwanted behaviours – usually with the teacher having no awareness of why this is a problem for the child.

It may sound very obvious, but I have found that it is best for them to be directly facing the learning board – this makes it easier for the child to see information, without the continual need to look around others or to turn their head to see. There are times, however, when working at a group table may not be conducive to concentrating on the task in hand. On such occasions, when the distraction of the group dynamic is just too much for the child with autism to be productive in work, I would suggest that they move to a workstation. This could involve the child facing a blank wall with the tasks laid out in front of them, or having a three-sided carrel surrounding the child so that they are visually focused on what is directly in front of them – this can be best positioned at the end of the group desk, or separately in a quieter corner of the classroom, and it could be called the 'concentration station'. It is good practice to ask the child if they are happy to do their work there, don't assume that this is best for them, without checking first.

So, as you can see, there are a lot of points to consider carefully when you're organising where to place the child with autism in your class.

May I also suggest that you do not change the child's seating position throughout the year – changes can be very difficult and confusing for them, which may result in unwanted behaviours. If they are wishing to move seats because they are having difficulty with a particular classmate, it is better to move *them* rather than the child with autism.

A further point to consider is concerned with another sensory aspect. Some children with autism may experience different reactions to temperature, so I would avoid having them seated too closely to a heat source, as they may overheat, but be unaware of this. They may then find it difficult to understand why you would suggest that they might wish to remove their jumper, and they may not co-operate with this. This could also result in unwanted behaviours.

So, to summarise, here are some key points for consideration when thinking about classroom seating position:

Avoid having the child:

- Sitting next to the door

- Facing windows/streams of light

- Being directly between others

- Being close to a direct source of heat

It is advisable to have the child:

- Sitting at the end of a table

- Being offered a cordoned off area for quieter, more focused learning

- Facing the learning board

- Being within sight of the door

Visual structures – wall displays

In my experience, children with autism can be very easily distracted by too much visual stimuli. Typically, children with autism are visual learners, and so, you would think that having a wall full of colourful displays and visual learning aids would be a good thing, yes? The answer is, not always.

Most classrooms are very bright, colourful and visually 'busy' environments with children's work proudly displayed alongside useful reminders, such as alphabet and number charts, times tables, maps and so on. Whilst most typically developing children can use these as points of reference as and when required, for some children with autism this can prove to be a challenge. They can find great difficulty in 'filtering' out what is necessary to read at any given time, and they may want to read and look at *everything,* when you are perhaps wishing them to focus on something else.

One young boy I taught was continually fascinated by the drawings on a poster depicting the alphabet. This proved to be problematic, in that he would only associate the letters with the pictures that they represented on that particular chart; so, for example, the letter 'a' could *only* be the beginning letter of the word 'apple' on the chart (and not any other word beginning with an 'a') as that was what was depicted, and if someone were to say '"a" for ambulance', then he would immediately correct them accordingly. Similarly, he would also say 'apple – that begins with "a"' each time he would read the word 'apple'. Now, I am not suggesting that you should immediately banish all such charts from the classroom – this would not be fair to the rest of the children, but I would urge you to be mindful of the use of such resources. You may find that they *can* cope with these displays and not be adversely affected; as mentioned earlier, each child with autism is different, and as such, may respond differently.

One word of caution: I have always found it to be a better idea to put up and remove displays with the child present. Most children with autism like to have predictability to their day, and so, knowing what is going to change visually, in advance, will help to reduce that uncertainty and possible anxiety.

I once heard a story about a teacher who had been working with his class on a rainforest theme. The children had been painstakingly making a beautiful wall display for weeks, showcasing their artwork of forest species, trees and so on. One day the pupils came in, and the display had been partially torn down by the teacher after the children had left for the day, in order to have them gain some appreciation of the devastating effects of deforestation in rainforests worldwide. Now, this was controversial, and, for obvious reasons, I would not recommend that a child with autism be subjected to a sudden change or shock such as this, as it would almost certainly cause undue stress and this could result in unwanted behaviours.

Visual structures – labelling and accessibility of resources

Just as you would for any other child in your class, it is helpful to have resources clearly labelled and easily accessible. If a child you were teaching had a physical disability, you would not seek to take away their walking aids or ask them to walk. A child with autism has a neurological disability, so making visual adaptations is equally as important to support *their* needs. Here are some tried and tested approaches that have worked for me.

The classroom environment

Cloakroom area – positioning: I would always suggest that the child with autism has their peg at the end of a line – this is helpful in two ways: firstly, it clearly marks out *visually* where they hang up their jacket and locate their indoor shoes, and secondly, it avoids the whole being 'squished' between others dilemma – this can be particularly stressful if other children are jostling to get to the cloakroom area at the same time. Some teachers I have worked with have allowed a child with autism to go out a few minutes before the other children – my only dilemma with this, is that the other children may begin to resent the 'special treatment' you are affording to wee Johnny that he can leave the classroom before everyone else, and this may unintentionally ostracise him from his peers.

Cloakroom area – identification of personal space: Most teachers of primary school children will have some sort of visual identifier to denote a child's peg space, e.g. Sammy will have a spider (this can also help with recognition of initial sounds). I would suggest that, for a child with autism, you should always try to incorporate their interests (these may alter throughout the year, so be prepared to make a couple of changes to this). Knowing that wee Johnny is very keen on Spiderman, you would have an obvious visual reference, and pictures of Spiderman are easily available copyright free on the Internet for you to print. Having a familiar character or favourite film/television show will always 'draw' them to their peg and make it a less anxious experience for them to locate it.

Cloakroom area – incidentals: It is a good idea to ask parents to write the child's name on their plimsolls in a gel fabric pen – this ensures that they always wear their own shoes. I have worked with some children who can be quite upset if someone else 'claims' *their* shoes as their own – marking the shoes in this way, prevents this from happening. You could also use clothes pegs to clip them together – this helps to show how they are worn and thus avoids putting them on the wrong feet (a common occurrence). Some children with autism can appear to be quite 'clumsy' when it comes to fine and gross motor skills. Putting on a jacket can be quite difficult, and so I suggest that if a jacket has a hood, that the child puts this on first, and this action will then give the jacket 'stability' to allow their arms to be placed correctly into the sleeves. I have lost count of the number of upside-down jackets I have seen over the years until I tried this strategy.

Toilet area

Within the toilet area, it is a good idea to have visuals displayed (at their height) to denote what is expected of them whilst they are there – obviously within reason. There are many good (and free!) visual resources that can be downloaded from the Internet that will help with toileting routines. These resources can help to focus the child on what to do, and to remind them to wash their hands when they are finished (hygiene can be problematic for some children with autism in terms of the sensory elements involved). It is useful to have a series of visuals displayed to denote the sequence of hand washing. It is also helpful to have a 'toilet' symbol on the child's desk so that they can show it to the teacher when they need to go – if this becomes an 'opt out' for the child, then perhaps you can place restrictions on its use; e.g. they can go on two occasions outside of the break times, and they should hand the card to you each time they go – when the cards are used, then the 'opt out' visits to the toilet are no longer available.

Lining up

Whenever children are ready to go out of class at break times, they will usually form an orderly line to do so. For a child with autism, however, this may not be an instinctive thing to do. Lining up is a social event, and children with autism may not inherently understand what is expected of them in such situations. I have found that what can work, is to place a sticker or piece of coloured tape on the floor, to signify where you want the child to stand – this can be at the front of the line or at the back – you will need to line the other children up first, to see the exact position of where it should go. It may be, however, that wee Johnny always wants to go at the front of the line and will not be happy if he is not always there. My suggestion is to have a rule about this – classroom rules can be very useful for teaching about appropriate social skills and behaviours to children with autism. I would, in these situations, have a visual chart with the names written in the order of the line, and the line then 'moves up' the chart each day of the week, so that in a typical month, wee Johnny will have at least one chance to be the line leader.

Defining areas and boundaries

For some children with autism, it can be problematic to identify physical boundaries within the environment. It is helpful to have visual signifiers to aid them with this. There are many ways in which this can be done, but it is always useful to have symbols to denote the different areas. There are lots of free images available online that you can download and print that would work well, e.g. a symbol of a computer on the door of the computer suite – this symbol should correspond to the one on any visual timetable you have – more on visual timetables later in this chapter.

Sometimes, when a child with autism is in a particular area, they may wander off, and so it can help to mark out the area physically, with coloured tape on the floor – showing *visually* (and reminding them verbally) that they should remain within that area.

Some children may also attempt to leave the classroom. If you place a 'no entry' sign on the *inside* of the door to show 'no entry' to the *outside* of the classroom, this can help to alleviate this. You may have to explain what the sign means, as it may not be familiar to them. Using a 'stop' sign can equally work well in this situation.

For some children with autism, however, they may take a very *literal* approach to the use of this sign, and may never want to leave the classroom, so be prepared to remove it, or give permission for *them* to remove it, should they need to exit the classroom legitimately, e.g. to go to the toilet, or to go on an errand.

Labelling resources

It is important for all children to have easy access to the resources that they will use in class. It also helps to have symbols/photographs of the objects on the front of storage trays. I find that it is also useful to have photographs of the contents within small cupboards printed, laminated and displayed on the *outside* of the cupboard, to denote what is *inside* – this prevents some children with autism opening the cupboard doors to check the contents. This has happened previously in one of my classrooms when one young child would continually open the door to have a look inside, and when I placed the photograph on the outside of the door, this behaviour stopped.

Visual timetables

If there is one thing you should really do for a child with autism in your class, it is to provide them with a visual representation of what their day will 'look like'. I cannot emphasise enough, the importance of having a visual timetable to give predictability and structure to their day. It is also beneficial to the other children in your classroom too.

I would begin with a classroom timetable. Templates for these are easily available free of charge from the Internet, but if you want to 'splash out' a bit, your school could perhaps purchase Boardmaker™ from Mayer-Johnson. This will have all of the symbols you would ever need.

When deciding upon a classroom timetable, or in fact *any* visual timetable, it is important that the child knows what the symbol or visual is meant to represent. It is pointless to have a beautifully appointed class visual timetable that causes confusion to the child, or is totally meaningless to them. By simply talking through the symbols, it will help to explain what each one represents.

Sometimes however, symbols just do not 'make the grade', and in these situations, I would always suggest that you use photographs, especially if there are items or events that you want displayed where commercially produced symbols are not available, e.g. a planned visitor to the class. This is especially helpful if another teacher will be taking your class in your absence, or if you have a regular visitor to the class who teaches a specific subject, e.g. a music teacher.

A classroom visual timetable should ideally be positioned where all children can see it. It should also be of a large enough size that children are not coming out of their chairs to see what is next.

Although most books on the subject of using a visual timetable will advise you to position it vertically, I prefer to position it horizontally, as children will naturally read from left to right, unless of course you teach in a country whose language is written vertically. Some people do, however, like their timetable displayed vertically, as it then resembles a list, much like a shopping list – your knowledge of the child's preferences will determine the best way to do this.

It is pointless, however, to have a visual timetable displayed if it is not being used correctly. I would advise that after each, let's call it 'event', is finished, it is either taken off of the wall, or turned around with the blank side displayed to signify that it is finished. In this way, the child with autism is given visual information on what is next, and this will give structure and predictability to their day. I would always finish the day with a generic image of 'home' and explain that this is the time that they can leave the school building.

So, how many 'events' should be displayed at any one time? The whole day? I would only suggest this for older children. For younger children, it is a good idea to have the morning displayed, up to and including lunchtime. During the lunch break, you or your classroom assistant, can *then* display the afternoon's events.

I would talk through the timetables (first the morning one and then, once lunch is finished, the afternoon one). This helps to give clarity to what the children will be doing, thus avoiding any confusion. Children without autism will also benefit significantly from seeing what their day will 'look like'.

Occasionally, unexpected events can happen. In these circumstances, I would suggest placing a question mark above the original event that this new event has superseded, explaining that we didn't know about this, and that this symbol means that this new event is a 'change', and reassure them that they don't need to worry about it. You could even call it a 'change card'. You could then replace this question mark symbol with one that you now know should go there, e.g. class assembly. If this is not possible (there is no symbol perhaps), then you can simply leave the question mark there. I find it is good practice to 'throw in' a question mark event at least once a month, as this helps the child with autism to become more familiar with changes occurring, as these can be extremely difficult for some children with autism to accept. I think it will help to make acceptance of change easier if the child with autism is given a pleasant 'change card' every so often, e.g. substituting an 'event' that they don't particularly enjoy, for one that they do.

Visuals in other areas of the school

It is helpful to have visuals in each of the areas that the child may visit during the course of the school day, such as the toilets, lunch hall, gym hall and the computer suite. If the child is new to the school, this will help to familiarise them with their new environment. Having these pictures/symbols/photographs on the visual timetable will make it clear where the child should be. Within these areas, a visual timetable could also help to give guidance, e.g. within the lunch hall, a typical timetable would have direct instructions on where the child should collect their tray and food, where to sit, and what to do/where to go when they are finished. This brings me beautifully to the next topic – lunch!

Ordering lunches

Some children with autism that I have taught have had dietary requirements that meant that they could not have gluten or casein in their diet; some also had allergies or food intolerances. Other children displayed sensory sensitivities with regards to the texture, taste and temperature of foods, and some did not like to have their food touching other food on their plate. Some would only eat 'branded' items, some were quite rigid in terms of the food itself, for example, there may have been meatballs on the menu, but if they did not taste like the meatballs that they knew and loved, then they *couldn't* be meatballs, and they wouldn't want to eat them. If a child with autism in your class has such dietary differences, then it's important that you know of these in advance – speak to the parents to ascertain if there is anything that could potentially become a problem for the child. If there are no difficulties with food, then I would always suggest that you have a copy of the menu that the school is providing for that day, in advance. This will ensure that there are no sudden surprises, but, if there are, then the question mark symbol will come in handy here. It is a good idea to take photographs of the meals, laminate them, and then have these displayed in the 'lunch' event on your visual timetable – letting the child know what choices they have. There is more information about dietary difficulties in Chapter 8.

Personalised visual timetables

Whilst it is very important to have a whole class visual timetable, it is equally important to have a personalised visual timetable on the desk of the child or children with autism in your class. Now, you may think that this would just be an unnecessary waste of your time, and that this is just to give you extra work, not so, and I'll explain why. First, if you are putting up a visual symbol depicting 'reading', not all of the children will be on the same book, and so it helps if you can show *visually* the book that the child with autism will be reading. Now, before you say 'I don't have time to take photographs of every book they will read, laminate them and put them on the personalised timetable', the answer to that is, no you don't, and I agree with you. However, if you can take a photograph of the logo of the reading 'scheme' or textbook, then this would give a good visual signifier of what the class 'reading' symbol means. You could also do this with their maths and handwriting books.

As with the class timetable, it helps to have somewhere to deposit the 'spent' symbols. A good idea is to use a small box with a lid that has a slit in the top, into which the symbol can be 'posted' when it is finished. The box can be personalised with stickers or drawings that the child chooses, and this should make it more appealing to them.

If having laminated symbols taped to their desk is too visually stimulating for wee Johnny, then, if he is a good reader, I would opt for the handwritten list of tasks to be done in the morning, and in the afternoon. These could be written on a laminated blank A4 sheet of paper with a whiteboard pen – he could simply cross off each task as it is completed. Older children with autism would perhaps cope better with this method of timetable, and it could also be more specific, as you could write down the particular books or pages that they should be reading. If you are a super duper computer 'whizz', then you could have their tasks for the morning and afternoon on a tablet or other portable electronic device – if your school is very lucky to have such equipment.

I have been in some classes where each daily task, in laminated small card form, is attached to a key ring that the child can access throughout the day. This is useful if they are out in the playground, as the appropriate symbol can be shown to them so that they know what they are to do upon their return to the classroom. It helps, too, if staff have the same key ring and can show the appropriate symbol, if the child is reluctant to return to class after break times, or, say, after gym. It is also helpful to use these visuals to bridge the transition between the morning and afternoon sessions.

Classroom rules

The first thing I would say about classroom rules, is that some children with autism can be quite 'rule-driven'. They will often be the classroom 'police officers' and tell you that wee Jenny has broken the rule about x, y or z. This can be perceived by the teacher that the child is keen to have another peer reprimanded. For a child with autism, however, there is often a distinct line between right and wrong, and very few, if any, 'grey areas'. It is important to have classroom rules and boundaries, but I would urge caution that, for example, if you say that there is to be no talking whilst working, you may find that you will be told that *you* are breaking the rule if *you* speak. Similarly, I have seen a rule where children were to 'keep your hands and feet to yourself' (to avoid a child being engaged in physical activity with another). This rule, however, will almost certainly be broken if another child *accidentally* touches a child with autism – this could be perceived by the child with autism as a violation of that rule. So, I would be very careful in how you phrase them. I would always stick to what *you would like to see* in behaviour, rather than what you *do not want to see.* For example, it is better to have 'quiet working' than 'no shouting out in class'. You can also have visuals to denote what 'quiet working' would look like – there are lots of good examples of volume control gauges online that have a sliding scale element. There will be more discussion about volume control in the next chapter.

Now it may appear that you will be spending an inordinate amount of time making up all of these visuals, but please be assured, you need only make all of these items on *one* occasion, and they can then be used throughout the year. It is not necessary to re-invent the wheel here. Your visual timetables should not change dramatically, unless you have, say, a school trip, and this will be discussed later in the book.

I cannot emphasise enough how important it is to use visuals, even when a child with autism has an apparently excellent use of spoken language. It is also important to note that when a child is coping well with using visuals, that you are not tempted to take them away from them. You may feel that in so doing, you are helping the child to 'move forward', but this could prove to be counterproductive, and the child may show regression in both understanding, compliance, and ultimately, this could have an adverse effect on their subsequent behaviour.

Suggested reading

Visual timetables: http://do2learn.com/picturecards/VisualSchedules/index.htm
Boardmaker™
www.mayer-johnson.com/boardmaker-software/

Chapter three
LANGUAGE AND COMMUNICATION

A typically developing child will learn to speak and understand verbal and non-verbal communication quite naturally. They will begin school life with a vocabulary that is enriched by their experiences, and they will be able to communicate with their peers to express themselves, request information, make comments about events, share information and, generally, be very sociable. For a child with autism, this may not always be the case. As mentioned in Chapter 1, one of the conditions for having a diagnosis of autism is that there are impairments with language and communication, which can include some, or all, of the following:

- Literal interpretation of language

- Processing of language

- Use of idioms and sarcasm

- Joint attention and 'Theory of Mind' (also known as 'Mind Blindness')

- Non-verbal communication, including the use of gestures, body language and eye contact

- Creative and imaginative thinking

- Flexibility of thought

- Social communication

- Listening to others' points of view

- Reciprocity (the 'give and take' of a conversation, knowing when to listen, and when to talk)

- Recognising and communicating feelings

This chapter will give you some practical strategies that will help to minimise these difficulties faced by children with autism in a typical classroom setting.

But, before we examine how children with autism may have difficulty with language and communication, it is important to examine how *you* communicate in class, the language you are currently using, and how you can adjust *your* communication style to meet the needs of children with autism in your classroom.

Literal interpretation of language

The first item on the list details how a child with autism may interpret language very literally. It may be that you have asked the 'triangle' group to come to the front of the class, however, wee Johnny might not think of himself as being a 'triangle' (I've actually had a child say to me, 'I'm a *boy*, not a triangle'), and so, I would suggest that you say, 'Johnny and the triangles, come to the front'. I think it is important if you are giving an instruction or making a request of a child with autism, that you say their name first, to ensure that they know that the instruction is meant for them directly – this avoids confusion and ambiguity. If there is another child in the classroom with the same name, I would say *both* of the child's names – forename and surname – just to clarify whom you are meaning. You may be using phrases like 'it's raining cats and dogs outside' or 'take a seat' (you may be asked 'where would you like me to take it?'). Be very explicit when giving instructions – this is so important. Also, take care when describing events, for example, I can recall a child who was told by his peer that he was 'wolfing' his lunch, at which point the child became visibly upset and corrected the boy, through tears, saying categorically that indeed he was *not* a wolf.

Difficulties with the processing of language

Some children with autism can demonstrate a delay in processing *your* language. If you were to examine the content of your language in a typical day, it would be fair to say that it is most probably of a very high standard. It is perfectly reasonable for a teacher to display an excellent level of vocabulary and good grammar with the children in their class; you would want to be a good role model, and display a level of language that you would like to see the children use. For a child with autism, however, this high level of language, coupled with a typical conversational pace, and a slightly elevated volume, can cause a great deal of confusion for them. It may be that they are struggling to cope with the content of the words, the syntax, the grammar, or a combination of all of these. They may also be struggling with the pitch of your voice, the volume, or the pace at which you are speaking. These are all areas that a child with autism may find difficult. Here are the most common problems I've come across, and strategies that I have used successfully to help children cope.

Child responds with 'no' when you are giving instructions

This is probably because you are giving instructions by asking a question – 'Would you like to get out your maths book?' – 'no' will always be the default response to such questions, if they really do not want to do it. I would alter how you phrase this, by saying instead, 'Johnny, it's maths time – you need your maths book'. Try to avoid *asking,* when you want to *direct* a child to follow an instruction.

Child appears confused and will not do as you are asking

This is usually because they do not understand what you are requesting of them. I would usually keep instructions to one or two key words, e.g. 'Johnny, maths time' rather than 'It's time for your maths work now, Johnny, get your book out and we'll get started'. It may sound like you are speaking to a dog, 'Johnny, sit, Johnny maths book' – but trust me, they will benefit from your keeping the language simple and concise. Now please bear in mind here that not all children with autism, as mentioned throughout this book, will have the same level of difficulty. It is important, therefore, to adjust the content, pace and delivery of your language to suit the needs of the child with whom you are working – some children with autism may appear to have a very good grasp of expressive language (speaking), but their receptive language (understanding) may not be at the same level, and therefore, they too, may need instructions broken down, in order to gain a better understanding.

Child is taking a long time to follow instructions or completes instructions after everyone else

For some children with autism, there can be a delay in processing instructions. As a matter of principle, it is good practice to wait for ten seconds or so, to see if the child begins to follow what you have requested. It can take this length of time to process instructions, however, I've actually known it to take longer than this. As a rule of thumb, I would avoid giving the same instruction repeatedly – this will only cause further confusion, as they will naturally try to process the instruction from the starting point again. Also, please do not be tempted to try to rephrase the same question in ten different ways; I have previously done this, with the best of intentions, thinking that I was helping the child, but it invariably only added to the confusion.

Child is not following instructions

It also helps if you keep instructions in the order in which they are meant to be done. For example, instead of saying 'It will be lunch time after you have tidied up', simply say, *first* tidy up, *then* lunch'.

Child covers their ears as if not complying with your request

This is probably because there is too much noise in the background and perhaps you have had to raise your voice to get this instruction across to the child. Try moving a little more closely to them and lowering the volume of your voice, or show them visually, using their visual timetable.

Use of idioms and sarcasm

These are areas of difficulty for many children with autism. Literal interpretation can also add to the confusion when idioms and sarcasm are used. Some children with autism will not understand if you are using phrases like, for example 'I'll be with you in a flash' or 'paint the person next to you' – now you can imagine what they may do next. There are specific books available that can help to explain idioms in greater detail to a child with autism, and these are very helpful. It might be an ideal topic for a piece of language homework, that the child conducts some research into some commonly used idioms. It would help just to be very mindful when you use them with your pupils and explain what you mean by them – better to teach the *meaning* of the idiom, rather than have a very worried or confused child.

With regards to the use of sarcasm, this is something that a lot of children with autism simply do not understand. Again, the literal interpretation of language can have an influence here, and if you say one thing but you mean the opposite, it may not make sense to them. Why would someone say something that they don't mean? And what they have said is supposed to be funny? Obviously, sarcasm does occur between peers, but again, it is important to try to teach the meaning of sarcasm to a child with autism by giving examples. Sometimes they can encounter difficulties with their peers when they cannot respond appropriately to a sarcastic remark from them, for example, if someone gets accidentally hurt by a child with autism, they may make a comment such as 'oh thank you very much, you've just hurt me!' – to which a child with autism may innocently reply 'you're welcome!' – you can see where this could lead.

Joint attention difficulties and 'Theory of Mind'

Joint attention is a social behaviour involving two people sharing an object, experience or time together. It happens very naturally with a typically developing child, and involves lots of good eye contact and the use of gestures such as pointing, body language and speech. Having joint attention is a main precursor for a child being able to learn from another person. For children with autism however, this may not be an instinctive behaviour, and the notion of, for example, enjoying sharing a story with a peer, may not be their idea of having a good time. On a practical level, especially with younger children, it helps if you can teach them the purpose of a pointing finger – I have lost count of the times I have used a pointing finger, and when I ask the child 'what is this?' (whilst pointing to an object), the response is invariably 'your finger'. So, it is important to say 'my finger is showing you ... can you see what it is showing you?' You could then ask for them to point to something. This may sound like quite a silly thing to do, but some skills just simply have to be taught, as a child with autism may not naturally acquire them.

Some people believe that the reason why there are difficulties with joint attention in children with autism, is because they have not developed a 'Theory of Mind'; in other words, they cannot put themselves in someone else's shoes and see the world from *their* point of view. It may be that *you* think that it is a lovely idea to share a story with wee Johnny, but it may be the last thing that he wants to do, and he expects that you should know what *he* is thinking. This is best exemplified in the 'Sally Anne' test (if you put these words into a search engine, you can see the test in action). The 'Theory of Mind' or 'Mind Blindness' theory suggests that children with autism may find it difficult to understand the thoughts and feelings of other people. Having little understanding of body language and other non-verbal means of communication can also add to this difficulty.

Whilst having little understanding of another person's point of view can be difficult for a child with autism, it can be equally frustrating to them if *you* cannot understand *their* needs or wants. This is especially true if they are unable to verbalise their feeling and thoughts to you, but rather, expect that you will just instinctively know how they are feeling, because *they* know how they are feeling, so therefore, *you* should know too. This can be problematic if a child is feeling unwell, or is anxious and unaware that they ought to share this information with you. Speaking with the child's parents is helpful in these situations as they will know the tell-tale signs that the child will display when they are unwell.

Comprehension difficulties

It is important to note that some children with autism may be able to read texts in print by 'decoding' the words, but may struggle to understand the underlying meaning, or to get the 'gist' of the story. This is the case when a child has 'hyperlexia'; there is more on this later in the book.

It can sometimes be difficult for a child with autism to undertake comprehension tasks where they have to interpret the feelings of one of the characters in a story. You can help them to understand what is required of them by using examples from familiar stories. You can also draw parallels with other examples that are meaningful to them, for example, if they enjoy, or have a fascination for superheroes, you can relate this to 'how do you think Batman would feel here?'

Another difficulty can arise when you ask a child with autism to predict what may happen next in a story. As with interpreting feelings, it is also helpful to teach the concept of prediction, by using familiar stories that the child knows very well. It is a good idea to stop and ask, 'what happens next?' Then, when you are asking for a prediction of what could happen next in an *unfamiliar* story, you can use this as an example of what you are expecting from them as an appropriate response to the question. Modelling, in this way, is a good strategy to help them understand what is required of them. In fact, modelling what you are expecting from a child with autism is an excellent strategy to use in lots of situations, especially with social ones.

Non-verbal communication difficulties including the use of gestures, body language and eye contact

When we talk about communication, we naturally think of speech as being the key method to pass a message to a recipient. There are however, many other, often subtle ways, to communicate with others. Using non-verbal communication such as body language and gestures are just two such examples, and these can be particularly difficult for a child with autism to interpret, and to use.

If you think of how many ways you can, for example, say 'no', let's have a look – 'definitely not', 'not a chance', 'no way', 'uh uh', 'not on your nelly', 'never' etc.… and those are just the *words*. Now let's add in the gestures – shaking head, shaking finger from side to side, turning your back, putting up your hand using a 'stop' gesture, folding arms. This, as you can imagine, could be very confusing for someone who has difficulty not only in processing what 'not on your nelly' actually means, coupled with your shaking your head. Why not just say 'no'? Opportunities should be given for a child with autism to learn about what different gestures can mean, what your body can 'say' to someone, and to have fun learning about these different ways in which you can communicate without using speech.

There are lots of games and books on the market to support learning about body language and the use of gestures, but, being a teacher, you might want to organise your own. It is a good idea to have the child look through magazines or newspapers to find interesting facial expressions and then try to group them according to their 'meaning'. Another game you could try, is to play 'pass the facial expression', and the person who 'receives' it has to tell the person 'doing' it what the expression/body language is conveying to them. This is an interesting exercise, as quite often a child with autism will come up with the complete opposite of what the expression/body language is meant to convey. If you're going to play this as a circle type game, then I would advise waiting until nearly the end of the game before you ask the child with autism to take their turn, as this will give them time to process what they are expected to do. Now, I am not saying that all children with autism will have difficulties interpreting facial expressions and body language, but for those who clearly do, it is a worthwhile exercise.

Using role-play is another good method of communicating different gestures – you could re-enact a particular scene of a play or story using only gestures and facial expressions, coupled with body language – no speech allowed – can the children guess the story, play or scene? I would suggest that you do this on the first occasion with a story or play that is very familiar to the child – think of it as an extended game of 'charades'.

Another good game is to match the gesture to the actual word – but you provide a bank of words that have the same meaning; for example, a 'thumbs up' gesture could mean 'well done' or 'ok' or 'good' and so on. This challenges the child with autism who will think that only *one* word can match only *one* gesture. This alludes again to the literal interpretation of words whereby a 'thumbs up' gesture can only mean 'good job' rather than 'that's great', because 'good job' is what the child heard on the first occasion they saw the gesture used. I have had many a child tell me 'it's not "well done", it's "good job"' or vice versa.

Creative and imaginative thinking

I think we should begin with 'knocking on its head' the idea that children with autism have no imagination – it is simply not true (Canavan 2016). Where I feel most people are confused here, is that there is a difficulty with *flexibility of thought* – being quite rigid in thinking, and having a desire for predictability and routines, in other words, not really wanting very much to change. This is entirely different to having no imagination.

Children with autism are some of the most creative and imaginative thinkers out there. Where children with autism have difficulty with this, is that they find it hard to put all of their ideas down on paper. This has more to do, however, with what is known as 'executive functioning' – how your brain organises your thoughts and feelings. I have had many a conversation with a child with autism who could take me on a metaphorical journey to a distant land where creatures have all sorts of weird and wonderful events happen to them, but trying to put that down into a logical sequence of events, with the correct syntax, use of pronouns, verb tenses, spelling, and of course, the dreaded handwriting, can all be a bit too much. Wee Johnny will not bother, thank you very much.

A good way of helping with this, is to record electronically what the child is trying to tell you, and then unpick it later to 'tease' the story out. I find that if your objective is to have the child write a creative piece of work, then you should focus on the *content* and not necessarily worry too much about the spelling or the neatness of the handwriting. In fact, if it would help, they could use software that will type directly from their speech – I'm sure you will find it online, teachers like you are very creative in finding the latest 'gadgety' software.

It helps if you give structure or 'bones' to the story writing process. A simple guide to what is expected would work wonders, trust me. Something like this would be good to try:

- Who?

- Where?

- When?

- What happens at the start of the story?

- What happens in the middle of the story?

- What happens at the end?

This structure would give more predictability to the task than simply saying that you are looking for a really good story with lots of imagination – all of this can be too vague, and some children with autism will really struggle with it.

Inflexibility of thought

As mentioned earlier, one of the main difficulties for children with autism is concerned with inflexibility of thought – this is, after all, one of the main defining features of autism, and without which, a child would not receive a diagnosis. This can manifest itself in many ways, some of which are listed here:

- Strict adherence to rules and routines – to the point where no deviation can occur without the child exhibiting significant behaviours.

- Inflexibility with times – only eating at set times and not a minute later, or earlier – this can also apply to bedtimes. I have had many a parent tell me that their child had been extremely upset because they could not be in their bed for *exactly* the same time as they had been on the previous night.

Let's examine some of these difficulties in more detail.

Inflexibility with eating

This typically occurs when a child with autism is only eating certain textures, colours or shapes of food. Perhaps they are only eating hard textures, or bland, soft food, or very spicy food (although this can have more to do with sensory differences than the inflexible element – sensory differences will be discussed in more depth later in the book). As well as the content of the food, where it is positioned on the plate can become quite 'fixed' also. Some children with autism are not happy to have food touch other food on the plate. Equally, some children will only want to drink out of a specific cup or eat from a plate that is of their preferred choice of colour. I worked with a child who would only drink from a blue cup. What I did to help to resolve this, was to 'mix it up' a little. What I mean by this, is that I only had available every other colour *but* blue, that particular day. Yes, there was a 'moment' when the child was not very happy, but he quickly accepted that it was good to have a drink from the yellow cup today, and I said that I would try to find a blue cup, but I might not be able to find one – I never did find one. I would not, however, suggest that you deliberately lie to the child – please don't *promise* wee Johnny something that you know you cannot provide. Sometimes, in situations such as this however, this approach might not work, and you can use other ways to help. You could use a 'first and then' approach with this problem – 'first a drink from the green cup, then a drink from the blue cup', reinforcing this notion that they will get to drink from the blue cup, but only after they have tried the green one first – this can sometimes work as the child will quickly realise that it wasn't so bad after all to have a drink from a differently coloured cup, to the one that they were expecting. Giving lots of positive verbal praise when they are successful in achieving this goal can be helpful too.

Coping with changes to routines

Another difficulty can arise when a child with autism expects strict adherence to the set routines: this can be especially problematic in class when sudden unexpected visitors arrive, or when there is a fire drill. In instances such as these, you can use the 'change' card. The notion of change, as mentioned earlier, can be a very difficult concept for a child with autism to accept, and it may therefore have to be *taught* to them. It is a good idea to start off with a good change, one that will bring great delight rather than great dread. For example, you could try to substitute an activity that you know the particular child does *not* like, usually handwriting, with a 'change' card of an activity that you know they *would* like. I would, however, urge caution here, because if you always have a 'change' card for a fabulous event, then they will quickly associate that card with something wonderful, as opposed to something like, say, a fire drill.

It is important, however, to teach what this card represents, and therefore, I would consistently use the key word 'change', so that when a 'change' such as a fire drill *does* occur, they are much more prepared for that event.

Fire drills can be practised with children with autism – it is important to communicate to them that it is *just* a practice, and you do this so that they are really good at leaving the building safely and quickly, should there ever be a *real* fire. If you communicate the reasons *why* these changes are happening, it will help them to make sense of them.

Difficulties with social communication

Next on our list is social communication. This is one of the main areas of difficulty for people who have autism.

So, what is meant by 'social communication'? Well, it is something that a typically developing child will learn without being taught. It is the communication that happens every day between peers in a classroom – social 'chit-chat', the sort of conversations that typically developing children will have naturally, but children with autism may not. It also involves interpreting the body language discussed earlier, reading facial expressions, understanding emotions, and so on. It also concerns knowing when to talk, when to listen, when it is not appropriate to interrupt, and when it would be acceptable to do so.

Children and adults with autism may find this incredibly difficult. As mentioned earlier, all of this is usually done very naturally (and quickly) with typically developing children. Children with autism, however, may need that processing time mentioned earlier, to understand what is being said, and how they could or *should* respond.

Let's look at some problems that the child with autism in your classroom may encounter with social communication.

Child interrupting frequently/shouting out at inappropriate times

In these instances, it is important to have some kind of visual cue that they are doing this, and that it is not acceptable. I suggest using a 'stop' sign (laminated and taped onto a lollipop stick) as a visual aid to indicate that they should stop talking. This, of course, would have to be demonstrated in a role-play situation beforehand, so that the child understands its purpose. It also helps if the child is then told what they *should* do instead – and so, for this, I have used a 'wait' visual (you can have the 'wait' sign on the reverse and flip it around). Most children with autism respond very well to visual cues such as this, as it gives them a sense of what is required of them. When you are ready to hear what they have to say, you can simply put away the 'wait' visual and speak to them (it's important to remove it visually before you ask them to speak).

Child using too loud or too quiet a voice in class

I have taught many children with autism who have either been very quietly spoken, almost non-verbal, non-verbal and some who have used a very loud voice in class.

For some children with autism, this is often something about which they have no awareness. Again, it is important to have a visual representation of what you are looking for in terms of an appropriate volume of voice in class, and a good way to do this, is to make a volume gauge. This can be done very simply, by having three levels of voice that you find acceptable – playground voice, group voice and partner voice – arranged in a circle, and having an arrow (made from card) attached by a paper fastener, that you move around to denote which volume you would like to hear at any given time. It is important to stress, that this has to be demonstrated to the child by saying 'I am now going to use a very *loud* voice', then shout 'hello everyone!' and then immediately move the arrow to 'playground voice' on the gauge. This should then be repeated with examples of the other two volumes. It is important to use this with the whole class if the general noise level is too high, as you are able to demonstrate *visually* where the volume 'stands' currently, and where you would like it to be. You can then ask some children to come out to demonstrate. I would ask wee Johnny to do this only after a couple of other children have done so.

Personal space issues

Sometimes, children with autism may stand a little too closely to their peers when speaking with them. They may also stare quite intensely, and this can turn some children off from having any kind of social communication with them. I have found that a simple Social Story™ (Gray 2018) can help with this problem. A Social Story™ is, put very simply, a way to explain and give guidance in a social situation that a child with autism may find challenging or difficult to understand.

Another practical way to solve this issue is through role-play – this can be achieved through drama or social skills lessons that focus on personal space, and how we feel when that space is 'invaded'. As part of the lesson, children find a partner and gradually move in towards them, one step at a time. When they feel that the child moving towards them is just *too* close for comfort, they can then say 'stop', and ask the other child to take two small steps back. It helps if the child who is feeling uncomfortable can explain how it made them feel. This exercise can also be practised in the gym hall, when the children are queuing up to go for lunch, or when they are waiting to go outside to play. The important thing to remember is that you are teaching the child with autism how *their* close proximity to their peers may be upsetting or offensive to those peers.

Similarly, staring can be problematic if a child with autism is deemed to be 'staring out' another child, as this can often be perceived (incorrectly) as aggressive or goading behaviour. Again, a similar lesson can focus on how staring can be viewed by others. You can also use mirrors to give examples of what a 'staring' face looks like, and they can practise changing this facial expression with your modelling of what would be more appropriate.

With younger children, and some older ones, it helps if there are physical boundaries that are visible (where possible). For example, having coloured tape on the floor to section off areas, can be very useful. Most gym halls have the floors already sectioned off for specific games, e.g. football, basketball etc. These pre-painted lines can be very helpful in guiding children with autism into appropriate spaces, without encroaching too closely on their peers.

Focusing on a particular topic of interest

Some children with autism have very intense interests in particular subject areas. I have worked with some children whose interests have ranged from sharks to Academy Award winners from 1955 to the present day.

Whilst it is very useful for you as a teacher that the children display such enthusiasm for their chosen topics, it can also be problematic in terms of how it is communicated by them in class. For some children, they may wish to talk about their favourite subject 'to the death', and they may be unwilling to accept any contribution from anyone else who may wish to participate in the conversation. Other children, again, can view this as the child being aloof or arrogant, as they are not being allowed to join in.

A good way to deal with such an incessant monologue about a subject (I once listened to every Oscar winner from 1955), is simply to say, for example, 'this Oscar talk is going to finish in five minutes' and showing the child a visual representation of this time, e.g. a five-minute sand timer. This gives predictability to the child, time to prepare to finish, and it also gives you time to get on with teaching the other children too! It may sound a bit harsh, but it does work, unless you really *do* want to hear about who won the best Oscar for Film Editing in 1955 (it was Gene Milford for 'On the Waterfront', in case you are curious!).

Reciprocity

This leads me very well into discussing issues around reciprocity, or, the 'give and take' of everyday conversations. This can be very difficult for children with autism, as it may not come naturally to them to know when it is an appropriate time to interject, or wait, and for how long should they wait. Such situations can be very stressful for them, and so it comes as no surprise that they may wish to opt out of communicating with their peers altogether.

A practical way of dealing with this issue in a group discussion is to use a visual to denote whose turn it is to speak and, therefore, whose turn it is *not* to speak. This can be done quite well using a 'speaker's card' or an object of reference that is connected to the discussion.

Another practical way of dealing with this, is to set a time limit for how long each person has to speak. You can use a sand timer for this, or a digital clock (a stopwatch would also work well).

For anyone who is interrupting, you can also use the 'stop'/'wait' card, and you can even ask the child with autism to use this to judge who is speaking for too long, or who has not spoken enough (you would only do this if you were very confident that they would be able to exercise a fairly good judgement of the situation).

Recognising and communicating feelings

This is an area that many children with autism find frustratingly difficult to understand. As discussed earlier, there are many, many words that mean the same thing, and so this is also true for expressing and understanding feelings – not only their own feelings, but also those of other children. How many ways can you say that you are happy? Have a think now, and I would guess you will probably have more than ten words to describe that feeling. That could cause a lot of confusion for some children with autism – which word should they choose? Is it the 'right' word? For some children, it may also be difficult to equate that word to a feeling – what makes one person happy, may make another very unhappy, so feelings are very subjective, and this is also difficult to understand for some children with autism – this harks back to the 'Theory of Mind', as discussed earlier.

On a practical level, therefore, it's best to keep it personal. If a child has a real interest or enthusiasm for doing something, say to them 'this makes you feel happy'. By doing this, you are verbally labelling the emotion that they are very obviously feeling. Similarly, if a child is visibly upset at something or someone, verbally label the situation with 'this has made you sad – you're crying'. Now, it may sound very obvious to you, and you may ask yourself why you should bother to do this, but it gives clarity to the meaning of the word, and they can associate the feeling with the word.

It is also useful to have a 'bank' of words to describe emotions – this can be done with the exercise you did when you thought of how many words you can think of that mean 'happy'. Children enjoy games like this, and it 'cements' the idea that there are many words that can have the same meaning.

I have previously asked children to keep an 'emotions diary' – writing down each day how they've felt and describing the situation that gave rise to that feeling. This can be a useful exercise in determining the emotional state of some children with autism, especially those children who appear quite passive but who may actually be feeling really anxious, and just do not want to talk about it, or who show it physically in their demeanour.

Recognising the emotions of others can often be particularly problematic for children with autism. I have worked with a child who, upon seeing another child visibly upset, would laugh. Now, on first inspection, it would appear that the child with autism was being particularly cruel, laughing at the other child's misfortune, but when I investigated a little further, I discovered that he was actually laughing at the fact that the upset child was grimacing (in pain), and he simply found the boy's contorted and red face to be amusing. He had no awareness that this was not a socially acceptable way to react, but the other children did not appreciate this, so it is easy to understand how his laughing may have appeared provocative and be misunderstood by the other children, causing further isolation from them. In such situations, it is best to model an appropriate way to respond, rather than simply to chastise the inappropriate behaviour.

A good way to gauge the emotions of others is through drama. Scenarios involving heightened emotions can be played out, and opportunities can therefore arise to label these verbally. Children can be asked to exaggerate their facial expressions to denote how they feel, and this can help children with autism to appreciate them more fully.

There are, of course, many commercially produced games, DVDs and computer programs that help children to understand and decipher emotions.

It is important to remember that this is a skill that may need a lot of practice.

Suggested reading

Language and communication: www.autism.org.uk/about/communication/communicating.aspx

Topics of interest: www.ambitiousaboutautism.org.uk/understanding-autism/behaviour/obsessions-and-special-interests

Recognising feelings: www.thetransporters.com/index.html

Chapter four

ACCESSING THE CURRICULUM AND WRITING INDIVIDUALISED TARGETS

For any teacher, it is important that the children in their class, whether they have autism, or are typically developing, can access the curriculum in a meaningful way to them. In order for this to happen, it is important to take into account a few important factors.

First, the learning styles of the children: visual, auditory, kinaesthetic, sensory, or a combination of some of these. The vast majority of children with autism whom I have taught, have been visual learners. With this in mind, the visual structures that were discussed in Chapter 2 are very relevant: classroom visual timetable, personalised desk timetable, 'concentration station', where appropriate, and good labelling of resources.

Second, lessons should always be differentiated to meet the *autistic* needs of your learners. What I mean by this is that written and verbal instructions should always be clear and unambiguous – too much information may overload, and too much complex language may confuse. Timescales for completion of work should always be flexible, as it may take wee Johnny a bit longer to process instructions, formulate his answer, and then tell this to you.

Many of the children with autism I have taught have had what could be described as a 'jagged' or 'spiky' profile – in a nutshell, they may have 'peaks' of ability in some areas, and 'troughs' in others.

It is important to remember that autism is a developmental disorder, and as such, children with autism may not follow a typical linear pattern of development with their learning.

The following are some areas of difficulty that can be faced by children with autism in accessing the curriculum.

Motivation to learn

For some children with autism, there may be no obvious reason why they should participate in learning, and they may, as a result, be unmotivated and unwilling to do so. One successful strategy to engage reluctant learners that I have used previously, is to use the child's interests as a platform to encourage participation. Examples of how you could do this with, for example, a specific interest in transport, could include the following:

- In language: writing imaginative stories about, for example, 'the day I went in a rocket to outer space', or a factual writing exercise listing the component parts of a bicycle, or perhaps preparing a small talk on their favourite method of transport

- In mathematics: compiling bar graphs of the different types of transport that the children in class have used that day to come to school, reading timetables, or counting with toy cars instead of traditional cubes etc.

It can also be extremely helpful and motivating for the child to have a visual symbol or photograph representing their favourite subject on their peg, on their visual timetable beside their name, on their communication diary for home, and at their 'concentration station'.

Another way to motivate pupils to complete tasks is to use the 'first and then' approach. This involves having the desired activity that will motivate the pupil as the 'then' part – this activity can only be done when they have completed the 'first' part, your choice of task for them to complete. Once a child with autism can see *visually* what is coming next, it should motivate them to complete what *you* want them to do. A big word of caution however, is that you cannot let the child down and say 'oh we don't have time to do what *you* want to do now, sorry' – this will immediately remove the trust that the child has in you and will undermine your credibility in their eyes. I would also caution that you must have the 'then' part given as soon as the 'first' part is completed – you cannot have them wait for any length of time before they can be allowed to have their motivating activity. When you use the 'first and then' approach, you could use a sand timer to denote how long they have to complete the 'first' part, and this could then be extended on the next occasion. For example, if you want wee Johnny to do his writing exercise for ten minutes, then you would use a ten-minute sand timer, and for the next time you would use a fifteen-minute sand timer, so he will still get to do his motivating activity, but it will take him a little longer to begin it. Similarly, you can increase the tasks you are asking him to do before he can begin it; for example, first writing, then spelling and finally, transport book.

Reward charts are also a good way to motivate children with autism, and you can personalise them with their favourite character or topic of interest. One young boy I taught was fascinated by numbers, and so, when it came to motivating him to complete his handwriting work (which was definitely *not* his favourite choice of activity), I would have his reward chart on his desk (beautifully decorated with numbers), and each time he would complete his handwriting work, he would be allocated time to play with the magnetic numbers (his favourite activity). Reward charts can also be used to encourage participation in non-academic subjects such as, for example, eating. I worked with one young boy who would receive a 'happy face' drawn on his chart for each time that he would attempt a new food. This worked so well, that by the end of the term, he had tried at least ten new foods, and was rewarded with spending extra time on the computer. If you make the reward visual, and exciting enough, then there is motivation, and therefore reason, for them to complete what you would like them to do.

Sometimes, 'reverse psychology' can work well to motivate. You could try saying 'I bet you can't finish that before the sand runs out' – sometimes this can work well but it all depends on the individual child.

Hyperlexia

Some children may come to school with the skill of already being able to read without being taught to do so, a very definite 'peak' in their profile. Parents are usually amazed and excited by this and will often see this as a very positive thing for their child to be able to do. And it is, but I have worked with children with this ability – hyperlexia – and whilst it is indeed impressive to hear a five-year-old child read aloud quotes from Shakespeare, when you dig a little deeper, and ask questions about what they are reading, it begins to 'fall apart'. In such instances, I prefer to call it 'decoding' the words, rather than reading, as reading, as you know, is a skill that transcends merely *deciphering* the written word.

Difficulties with comprehension

With hyperlexia, there is often a difficulty with the comprehension of the text, and as mentioned earlier, understanding the 'gist' of the story or piece of writing (Chia & Kee 2013). You can see, therefore, where difficulties can arise, when you begin to mention to parents that wee Johnny, who 'reads' Shakespeare, requires some support with his reading.

When there is a difficulty in this area, you can use the child's decoding skills to explain what you are expecting from him in the lesson. For example, if he has read a story to you, and you know that he just doesn't 'get it', then you could write down three possible answers and ask him to read which one he thinks will best describe the story to someone else. To use a very simplified example: if the child has been reading a story such as 'Hansel and Gretel', you could ask 'Is it... 1. A story about a boy and a girl lost in the woods?', or 'Is it... 2. A story about a boy and a girl who are on their way to the shops?', or 'Is it... 3. A story about a boy and a girl who are having a picnic in the woods?' Now obviously, you would differentiate the level of complexity of the questions according to the needs of the child, and their level of understanding, but you can see how this could help to explain what you are looking for in terms of his comprehension of the text that he is so eloquently 'reading'.

High ability with numeracy

Some children with autism may not exhibit skills in reading, but they may display a strong ability with numeracy. I have taught children whose numeracy skills were far beyond their years and were astonishingly impressive at a very young age. One young boy could identify written numerals into the hundreds of thousands at five years of age, but he required differentiated support as he was very far ahead of his peers.

For children who have such extraordinary aptitude with numeracy, it would make more sense if they could be taught alongside peers of a similar ability. This may mean that they won't be working alongside their age and stage peers but may have to work with older children who are doing similar work. I would encourage this, but it is best to facilitate this without causing distress, as moving the child with autism to another classroom could cause anxiety and, possibly, later school refusal. It would be better, therefore, to ask one or two of the older children to come to *your* class to work within an environment that is already familiar and comfortable for the child with autism (this can sometimes be referred to as 'reverse inclusion'). Obviously, this would have to be in agreement with all parties involved, including parents.

Handwriting difficulties

Other difficulties can arise for children with autism who may have difficulty with handwriting. Again, I would urge common sense here, and if it is not the quality of the handwriting that you are seeking to teach and assess, then I would not make a big fuss about the written presentation if the subject matter were understood well. Answers can always be scribed by a teaching assistant (where possible), or can be recorded electronically, thus taking away the pressure of a perfect presentation that some children with autism place upon themselves. I once worked with a child who was continually erasing written work as it did not look like print to him, and it was, therefore, in his opinion not good enough.

Other practical strategies to help with handwriting can include using pencil grips to encourage a tripod hold, using pencils or pens that make marks more visible (some children with autism have a very light touch when writing, and it can be difficult for them to see what they've written) and having lined paper available, as writing on lines gives more structure than writing on a blank sheet of paper. For younger children with difficulties with handwriting, you can try 'writing' in sand, 'gloop' or shaving foam (check beforehand that they do not have any allergies to the materials). It can also be helpful to write on coloured paper, as white can be too bright for some children with autism. It can also help children if you write down, for example, spelling words, using a yellow highlighter pen and they simply write on top of that – this gives a good example of what you're looking for, and also gives them support to practise writing the words correctly. Within the highlighted letters, you could also draw arrows to demonstrate the correct letter formation.

Fine motor skills difficulties

This is a common problem for children with autism and can quite naturally be linked to the difficulties mentioned with handwriting. There are many ways to help with this issue including:

- Painting using fingers

- Using hand and finger puppets

- Threading beads onto laces

- Making 'sausages' and 'peas' with play dough

- Posting small coins into a piggy bank

- Using scissors to cut in straight lines, zig-zag lines, curves and circles (in that order of difficulty)

- Picking up little items with oversized tongs and tweezers

- Popping bubble wrap

- Having items that you can pull and push apart using two hands simultaneously

It is a good idea to have daily practice of one of these activities to develop their fine motor skills.

Copying work from the learning board

One of the problems you could encounter is when you ask a child to copy text that is written on the learning board. As mentioned earlier, it is helpful for the child with autism to be directly facing the learning board. Some children with autism, however, can find it very difficult to look at the board, look back to their paper and then write down what they have seen, as they can easily lose sight of what they've previously read. You could, in such instances, try writing each line in a different colour – this will make each one stand out from the rest, and it should then make it easier for the children to copy onto paper.

Colour coding, in general, works well to make distinctions between different events, for example, on timetables: you can have morning work coloured blue, and afternoon work green, or breaks highlighted in yellow.

If you have one of those fancy new electronic boards, then I would suggest only putting up one line at any one time, e.g. if they are copying down mathematical sums, only have one row of sums shown at a time rather than a whole board full, but if the rest of the class is waiting for wee Johnny, then give him his own smaller whiteboard.

Transitions

Transitions can happen between lessons, during lessons, between breaks, and sometimes unexpectedly during the day, for example fire bells or unexpected events. These can be extremely challenging for a child with autism, especially if such events are unannounced.

Having visual timetables for the class and for individual desks is so important to signify when these natural transitions occur, e.g. when one subject finishes and another begins. You could, however, have mini schedules that will help with transitions *during* lessons; e.g. for 'language' time, you could break this down even further to incorporate all of the tasks that you would like the child to complete within 'language', e.g. reading book, spelling, comprehension sheet etc. You could also have a 'finished' sheet to suggest activities that the child could do, should they finish quickly. I have found that when children with autism are unsure about what to do next, it can be stressful for them and this can often lead to difficulties with knowing how to respond appropriately.

As well as visual symbols on their timetable, you could also try to use a visual object of reference. You could say, 'In five minutes, we will be going to the gym hall' and then show them a small piece of equipment relating to what they will be doing, e.g. ball or skittle.

Having a visual representation of time passing between different activities is also helpful. I have seen bells and buzzers used, but I find that these can make some children with autism quite anxious in the anticipation of the noise. I prefer visuals such as sand timers, or electronic timers that are widely available on the Internet that depict red, amber and green as a visual 'countdown' to when the activity is nearing its time for completion. These can be pre-set by you and are a good visual way to denote the time required, and thereby give the child a less stressful countdown than a buzzer going off beside them, especially if they have auditory hypersensitivity.

A big transition event happens when the child has finished primary school and is heading off to secondary school. A lot of planning and preparation needs to happen for this to have a successful outcome for any child with autism.

Below is a list of helpful suggestions to ensure a smooth transition for a child going to a new school environment.

- Having planned visits to the new school with a familiar adult (this could be the parent, classroom assistant or teacher)

- Child taking photographs of the new environment and all of the areas within the building that would be pertinent to them

- Where possible, having photographs of the teachers and staff who are relevant to them

- Child making a book about their new school and labelling the photographs that they have taken

- Doing all of the above far in advance of the first day (it is helpful if it can be done over the Summer holidays, as this will give the child lots of time to assimilate the information and be better prepared for the new environment)

- Creating a timetable for the first day at their new school – this is especially helpful if they have to attend a special assembly

- Preparing a child 'passport' to hand over key information to the receiving school. This could include the following information:

  o Photograph of the child

  o Academic work and ability

  o Learning style

  o Behaviour management strategies that have been proven to work successfully, e.g. what motivates them

(Continued)

- Sensory needs

- Dietary needs/preferences

- Medical needs

- Any other pertinent information to support a smooth transition, e.g. the child's special interests

- Having a meeting with key personnel to discuss all of the above in advance of the child starting their new school – this will give an opportunity to discuss all of the child's requirements and hand over key information. This meeting should involve the child's parents and all professionals currently supporting the child. It would also present an opportunity to discuss which strategies are currently working well to support the child, with the expectation that this will continue in their new school

Writing individualised targets

If the child with autism that you are teaching is not able to access the curriculum as well as their mainstream peers, then they will require support for their learning. The best way to do this is to set targets for the child and develop strategies that will help to achieve them.

It may well be that wee Johnny is actually accessing the curriculum fairly well and does not present with difficulties in his academic work, but he may have difficulties in other areas of the curriculum – in, for example, his social skills – and he may require individualised targets to address his difficulties within this area.

Very often in my teaching career, I have seen young children who have been academically very able, but who have lacked in areas that a teacher would not usually target – for example, co-operative working with their peers. It is important to recognise these types of difficulties, and to target them with strategies that will help the child to progress. After all, you are teaching the *whole* child, not just the academic side of their being. Very often, it is the skills that underpin the learning that need to be targeted, in order to make the child access the curriculum more meaningfully.

Any targets that you write should be viewed as a working document, and not just a piece of paperwork that goes into a forward plan as part of a 'box-ticking' exercise.

Ideally, targets should be evaluated termly, but obviously this is not 'set in stone', as the child you are teaching may have achieved their targets sooner than this, and in these instances, it would make sense to set new ones, if required. Some children may take longer than a term to achieve their targets, as they may require extra time to consolidate key concepts.

Now I know that you are very busy and will appreciate having a bank of targets and strategies, and so I will detail a few helpful suggestions for areas that may require targeting, and some general strategies that could be used to help to achieve them.

These targets are not written with any specific chronological age of child in mind. It is important to note that some children may not be operating at the same level as their typically developing peers. As such, these targets are written to cover a variety of stages within primary, and therefore, should only be viewed as examples of some good ideas.

Language and communication

Attention and listening

Target: To participate in listening to a whole class story on three out of five occasions

Strategies:

- Ask the child to sit at the front of the large group – this will help to avoid being distracted by people in front of them

- Use familiar, favourite stories to encourage participation

- Use interactive books that require the child to come out to the front to lift the flap or press a button to make a sound

- Ask the child to come out to the front to turn the pages or hold the book

- Use short stories that only involve sitting for five minutes and then gradually increase the length of the story as the child copes with sitting in a large group

(Continued)

- Give praise, stickers or rewards when they have sat well
- Use the 'first and then' approach to show 'first' story, and 'then' to indicate the child's preferred choice of motivating activity

Resources:

- Familiar stories (large books)
- A range of book types, e.g. interactive, lift-the-flap, press a button to make a noise etc.
- Stickers/reward chart as a motivator
- 'First and then' pictures of story and motivating activity that the child moves on to after the story

---

Target: To share a focus of attention with an adult on a task for at least ten minutes

Strategies:

- Sit alongside the child when working – this will be less confrontational to them
- Model what is expected of them and use visuals to support what they *should* be doing – e.g. 'good sitting' or 'good listening' visuals
- Follow their lead, and support and extend their participation by adding to it with your suggestions
- Use clear and consistent language, and keep it brief and succinct
- Allow for processing time
- Use a ten-minute sand timer to denote *visually*, the passing time

Resources:

- A ten-minute sand timer
- Completed examples – e.g. in handwriting

Target: To follow two-part instructions on four out of five occasions

Strategies:

- Say the child's name and gain eye contact (where appropriate) before giving the instruction to ensure that the child is aware that the instruction is meant for them

- Use clear and concise language that is unambiguous

- Keep language simple and in the present tense, e.g. avoid saying 'I would like you to...'

- Give the instructions in the order that they are meant to be carried out, e.g. 'go to the office and hand over this letter", rather than "hand over this letter at the office'

- Give at least ten seconds for the child to process the request (and avoid repeating the instruction)

- Ask 'what have you to do?' – if they don't know, *then* you can repeat

- Show visuals or objects of reference to support your request, e.g. photograph of office and letter

Resources:

- Photographs or visual symbols supporting the request

Reading

Target: To answer questions relating to the text on three out of five occasions

Strategies:

- Provide the child with opportunities to look at books with the words covered up by a sheet of paper blu-tacked onto the page so that they have to *look at the pictures* to tell what is happening in the book (some children with autism may think that they simply have to read the text to you as a response)

(Continued)

- Model a correct 'ask and answer' response with another member of staff, or another child
- Give the child three possible answers, and they have to deduce which one is correct
- Gradually increase the complexity of your questions, e.g. begin with 'what' and 'who', and then increase the difficulty by asking 'when', 'how' and 'why' questions as these will not be so visually obvious

Resources:

- A variety of books, e.g. reading books, story books etc.
- Blu-Tack
- Key adults (for modelling purposes)

Target: To recognise and read the sight vocabulary from the reading book, in and out of context

Strategies:

- Provide the child with a set of laminated key vocabulary words and corresponding pictures
- Have the words written or typed onto yellow paper
- Use sensory games to find the words, e.g. putting the key words in a small box containing shredded paper and matching them to the corresponding picture cards.
- Provide interactive electronic games containing the words

Resources:

- Key vocabulary words (laminated)
- Yellow paper
- Corresponding pictures (laminated)
- Box of shredded paper
- Interactive electronic games

Writing: handwriting

Target: To form recognisable letters and words legibly when writing

Strategies:

- Ask the child to practise 'writing' the words in gloop, sand and shaving foam

- Provide a variety of writing materials including extra dark writing pencils and coloured pens

- Use pencil grips to encourage a correct hold

- Model correct letter formation

- Use yellow highlighter marker to write out the letters onto which the child will superimpose their letters – you can also draw arrows depicting direction within the letters in contrasting black ink

Resources:

- Trays for containing 'writing' materials

- Cornflour and water for gloop

- Shaving foam

- Sand

- Variety of writing materials

- Pencil grips

- Yellow highlighter pen

Writing: functional writing

Target: To write instructions on making a sandwich, in a clear and organised manner.

Strategies:

- Provide the child with lots of good examples of what a functional piece of writing should look like, e.g. recipes and instructions

(Continued)

- Detail what you are looking for in terms of their input – how many 'steps' in the instructions do they need to write? Be as specific as you can be
- Use the child's interests to motivate them to participate, e.g. if the child has an interest in trains, then they could be asked to write instructions on how to prepare a sandwich for a train journey

Resources:

- A variety of examples of functional writing, e.g. recipes, instructions etc...
- A selection of writing materials and paper

Maths and numeracy

Target: To count, order, read and write numbers to twenty

Strategies:

- Provide concrete resources to aid understanding, e.g. cubes, counters or items that the child has a specific interest in, e.g. cars
- Provide opportunities for matching quantities of objects to corresponding amounts using magnetic numerals
- Use sensory preferences, e.g. if visually stimulated, give the child a torch to indicate x amount of flashes
- Ask the child to hand numerals to children in a queue to indicate their position in the queue
- Use tactile resources such as gloop to 'write' numerals
- Use favourite ICT programs to reinforce numeracy to twenty
- Use games to reinforce quantities, e.g. dominoes

Resources:

- Cubes, counters, pegs or toy cars for counting
- Magnetic numerals

- Torch (if child is visually stimulated)

- Gloop

- Computer programs for counting

- Dominoes

Properties of shapes

Target: To recognise and name 2D shapes and 3D objects

Strategies:

- Use real 3D objects

- Use the child's interests to make associations with the shapes

- Use modelling clay or play dough to make the shapes

- Make the shapes with their bodies during gym lessons

- Provide games to enable shape matching

- Organise a shape 'hunt' around the school

- During art lessons, draw shapes using a variety of media

Resources:

- 3D objects – these can be the commercially produced ones, or use real 3D objects such as an empty shoe box for cuboid or empty tube of sweets for cylinder

- Modelling clay or play dough

- Games for matching shapes, e.g. 'Dotty Dinosaur'

- Art materials for drawing or painting shapes

Money

Target: To use coins to pay for items up to the value of £2

Strategies:

- Use real coins! Some children with autism may not understand why you are not using real money

- Teach equivalence of coin value by *visually* showing all of the coins that make specific amounts, e.g. ten x 1p coins is the same amount as one x 10p coin etc

- Set up a class 'shop' to use the coins

- Provide opportunities to use coins, for example, buying items on community visits to the shops

Resources:

- Real coins

- Class 'shop'

- Visits within the local community to purchase items

Time

Target: To tell 'o'clock' times using an analogue clock

Strategies:

- Use real clocks and watches

- Ask the child to set the hands on the clock to show specific times that you request

- Play 'What's the time Mr. Wolf' as a warm-up during gym lessons – using a large analogue clock face to depict the time

- Make reference to the clock throughout the day to ask the children to tell you what time it is (on the hour, every hour)

Resources:

- A variety of real analogue clocks and watches

Social skills

Target: To develop self-confidence

Strategies:

- Provide opportunities to talk about what the child is doing

- Offer help with activities when required

- Intervene in difficult situations

- Ask the child to take photographs of good work that they have completed, so that they can talk about it, and be reminded of their good work

- Ask them to take photographs of their favourite objects or events, so that they can talk about them confidently

- Provide them with an opportunity to have a mini project on their favourite subject

- Provide regular opportunities for them to talk about their favourite items in a small group

- Provide opportunities for them to reflect on their successes, achievements and talents

- Have a group/class points system or reward chart to promote success

Resources:

- Camera

- Peers for circle time

- Group/class points system

- Reward chart

Target: To share resources and take turns

Strategies:

- Create opportunities for sharing and turn taking, e.g. during games, when sharing a book with another child, during gym lessons

- Encourage participation in turn taking board games, e.g. lotto games

- Place the lid of the game beside the person as a visual cue to show whose turn it is now and next

- Keep language clear and consistent e.g. "Simon's turn, Johnny's turn"

- Use a sand timer to denote the duration of their turn

- During daily routines and favourite activities, try to encourage sharing, turn taking and waiting for a turn

- Where possible each child has a short turn each, e.g. using the computer

- On a laminated sheet beside the resource, have a list of names that can be crossed off, indicating who has already had a turn

Resources:

- A variety of games for sharing, e.g. board games, lotto games

- Sand timer to denote duration of turn

- Laminated board

Target: To cope when overwhelmed

Strategies:

- Build relaxation time into the child's daily routines – a quiet five minutes at the end of the day reading a favourite book, can be a good way to de-stress

- Provide a visual symbol for the child to communicate to the teacher that they require 'time out'

- Provide a quiet space (this could be a corner of the classroom), with little visual stimulus present

- Discuss (when the child is calm) some strategies that they could use to become calm, e.g. if they enjoy visual stimulation, then looking at a lava lamp or water and glitter within a bottle may de-stress them. If they are stimulated by their auditory sense, then listening to a rainmaker musical instrument or water running may perform a similar function. Equally, they may become calm by using a fidget toy, or popping bubble wrap

- Encourage deep breathing to slow down the child's heart rate, asking them if they can feel their heart beat slowing down

- Encourage them to count backwards from ten, letting them know that the aim of this, is to get to a calm state by the time they reach zero

- Scrunch up/rip some waste paper

Resources:

- Visual to denote 'quiet time'

- Resources that will calm the child – this will be dependent upon the child's needs – speak to parents about what works at home

- Waste paper for scrunching or ripping

Suggested reading:

Hyperlexia: www.autismkey.com/hyperlexia/
Pencil grips: www.brightideasteaching.co.uk/Pencil-Grips
Transitions: www.autism.org.uk/professionals/teachers/transition-tips.aspx

Chapter five
BREAKS AND UNSTRUCTURED TIMES

For any child with autism, break times, and in fact any time that is unstructured, can prove to be problematic, and this can cause anxiety, and occasionally, some inappropriate behaviours.

When I say 'break time', I am talking about the morning interval/recess/playtime between the start of the school day and lunchtime, and the period after lunch before afternoon lessons begin. In some schools, there may also be an afternoon break.

'Unstructured times' refers to those times in the school day where events are not 'scripted', for example when the school photographer comes, unexpected visitors arrive, the fire bell sounds or when there is a whole school assembly.

Let's look firstly at break times. For most typically developing children, break times provide an opportunity to socialise with friends, play games, run around and generally have some 'down time' before lessons begin again – a chance to unwind. For many children who have autism however, this may not be the case. Let's look at some possible reasons why this might be so.

- For some children with autism, break times do not have a 'script' that they can follow – what do they do? – this can cause real confusion and anxiety

- The noise levels in any playground can generally be quite high. Children are naturally excited to be outside and can shout to their friends and be quite loud. This can be very overwhelming for some children who may have hypersensitivity to sounds, and the noise can hurt their ears

- The whole idea of a social setting where all children come together to play can be quite difficult for someone who has a social communication disorder, and as such, the 'chit-chat' and everyday conversations that children have, can be difficult to follow

- Inclement weather days – this may involve a change to the usual routine of going outside to play

So what can you do to help if a child does not cope with break times? Let's analyse these issues a little further.

Not having a 'script' to follow

This can be remedied in a variety of ways. Firstly, you could give some structure to the break time by introducing a quiet area with set activities in the playground. This needn't be difficult to do – you could have an area equipped with some desktop games, a small pop-up tent that could contain jigsaws and books, or you could give skipping ropes and balls to the child as visual objects of reference to indicate what they could do. Perhaps, if your school has a healthy budget, you could consider a small sensory playground for children who find the main playground a little too overwhelming. I have witnessed good examples of this type of play area that have small climbing frames, wind chimes, mini trampolines (built into the grass) and spinning objects that reflect the light. You could have mirrors placed on the wall, too. Of course, these items all cost money, but it is worthwhile, should your school have the finances to support it.

Another way to help with what the child is meant to do during break times, is to give them structured examples of what is on offer in the playground. It may look like this:

You can choose from the following (have visuals or the actual objects themselves displayed):

- Play with balls

- Play with skittles

(Continued)

- Play with a buddy

- Play with skipping ropes

- Take a book outside to read

- Walk or run around outside

- Explore inside the play tent

Offering a child with autism some concrete examples of what they can do, may encourage them to participate, but for some children, they may just simply want to spend a little time on their own to 'let off some steam'. I would always argue that they should be allowed to do this; after all, we should not be trying to 'shoehorn' children with autism into following our societal script if they are unwilling or uncomfortable with this.

Noise levels

There are practical ways that you can alleviate the noise levels for a child who has hypersensitivity to sounds. One of the ways you can do this, is to allow the child to wear a set of ear defenders to nullify the noise. This can be very effective, but bear in mind that they may not hear the bell when break time is finished, so a visual cue – a few minutes near to the end of break time such as a sand timer or tapping on your watch to indicate 'two minutes' – would be a good idea. Similarly, if ear defenders are too bulky and draw too much unwanted attention, then the small ear pieces that are widely used for listening to music can be put into their ears for much the same effect (these can be playing their favourite tunes or audio books, if allowed in your school).

Another way to combat the often very high noise level, is to section off a quieter corner of the playground and call it a 'chill zone'. This can be where your pop-up tent is located, and where noisy children are not encouraged to enter. You could even have a sign with someone shouting with a red diagonal line drawn through it to indicate this visually.

Social communication difficulties

This could be the most challenging aspect for a child with autism to face when they have break times. There are several ways that you can promote their friendships with their peers, here are some examples

- Assigning playground 'buddies'. These can be older pupils who are responsible for guiding them around the playground and encouraging them to play with other children. It would help if these children were visually obvious as 'buddies' by wearing either a hat or badge to signify their role. I would, as a classroom teacher, make this a very responsible job, and have 'auditions' for the role – this is something that you want pupils to *want* to do, not to be something that they feel burdened with doing. Girls are usually very nurturing and want to 'mother' the boys. Now, before you call the sexist police, I am only referring to my experiences with wee girls who just want to make sure wee Johnny is fine, do up his shoes for him, get his jacket for him. These are kind deeds, well meant, but not always helpful for wee Johnny to progress independently. I would always suggest having a good 'bank' of buddies available, as you do not want children with autism to become too dependent on the same child each time they go out to play. I also think it is very important that the buddies have time to themselves, and so it would be helpful to have them on a rota system, where they are only assigned to do one 'shift' per week. This keeps it interesting for the buddy, but also takes away the pressure from them. There needs to be a set of rules to which buddies should adhere. You and the child with autism can determine these. For example, you may wish to have one rule that if the buddy at any time feels unsure what to do, that they should approach an adult for advice.

- Having a 'meet and greet' bench (one from your gym hall would suffice here) where children who want to socialise, but are not confident in approaching other children, can be seen and encouraged to come and play by staff in the playground. Buddies can be assigned to help with this role, too.

- Social Stories™ and Comic Strip Conversations, are excellent strategies for teaching a child with autism about appropriate playground conversations. There are many good examples available in the 'Suggested Reading' section at the end of this chapter.

- Similarly, your playground 'buddy' could model conversation 'starters' and then try to encourage the child with autism to try it out with another child.

If staffing levels allow, it can be a good idea to run lunchtime clubs. These are a productive way for a child with autism to occupy their time, whilst also giving an opportunity for them to socialise with their mainstream peers. It is best if the club is not based on anything too academic, as this could put off some children. I would, where feasible, incorporate the child's interests here. For example, if the child with autism in your class is particularly good at drawing and enjoys participating in arts and crafts, then this would be a good choice of club. Similarly, if they enjoy playing chess or board games, then having a 'games' club would work well. I have seen computer lunchtime clubs where the child with autism excelled and was more included by his peers when they viewed how talented he was on the computer.

At the start of the term, you could have a class vote on which club to run, but you needn't have just one club if you have the facilities to accommodate more. I would suggest though, that you limit how frequently these clubs happen, e.g. once or twice a week only, as children with autism may wish to choose that option every day, and they may not wish to participate in any outdoor activities.

Inclement weather days

One of the most common problems can occur when the weather is inclement, and outside play is not available. Usually the children remain indoors supervised by older pupils. It would help if an indoor play box could be available, from which the children could choose items to play with inside the classroom. Perhaps you could provide a list of jobs that the child with autism can do (they may actually prefer this), for example, water the plants, collect and sharpen the pencils etc. For some children with autism, it may be difficult to be inside at break times, as there is, first, a change to their normal outside play routine and, second, there are different people supervising them.

With inclement weather days however, planning and preparation are key. With modern technology, it is not difficult to determine what the weather will be like in advance, and so, armed with the knowledge that it may rain today, you can prepare the child with autism verbally, and support this with visuals early on in the morning, so that it comes as no big sudden change that they may be remaining indoors at break times. I would also suggest having a rain/snow/fog/windy visual above 'break time' in advance, where possible, so that the child will know, visually, where they are to be at that time.

There may be times however, when the weather can change suddenly, and without warning. At times like these, your school would normally have a system in place to denote either audibly (x number of bells rung) to indicate that it's time to come in, or there may be a whistle blown. Whatever system you have in place, don't always assume that the child with autism will either know, or remember this, and so call upon the 'buddy' or playground assistant to tell them either verbally, or use a visual to communicate to them that the remainder of the break will take place indoors.

Unstructured times

As with break times, the key to having a child with autism understand what they are meant to do, is to explain to them and support this visually. So, what is meant by unstructured times? I'm referring to those times where typically developing children will often squeal with delight, such as 'golden time' (where children are rewarded with good behaviour all week by having 'down time' on a Friday afternoon), 'choosing time' (where children are given free choices) or where visitors come to the class and may wish to speak to the children, e.g. when parents visit the class to talk about their job, or if a dental nurse comes in to talk about tooth brushing skills or oral hygiene.

These types of visits can be problematic for children with autism for many of the same reasons as break times, but break times, however, have predictability in terms of their time frame, whereas such visits to the class can perhaps be shorter or longer than anticipated, and this can cause anxiety for some children with autism.

One way of dealing with this problem is to try to create some predictability, where possible. For example, you should know in advance if someone is coming to make a visit to your class to talk to the children. You could have a photograph of them that you have taken previously, displaying it on the visual timetable to indicate visually who is coming into the class today. Where possible, I would let the visitor know in advance that they will have a set amount of time to speak with the children/answer questions – you could facilitate this by saying 'Mrs. "So and so" will be speaking with us about teeth cleaning for twenty minutes, so please listen carefully as she may ask you some questions'. If possible, your visitor could signify that the talk will be ending soon by saying 'I will be finished in five minutes, and then you can ask me questions'. This will give reassurance to the child with autism that there will be an ending soon, and thus alleviate any anxiety that they may have.

Another difficult time for pupils with autism can occur when there is an element of 'free choice' in the day – this could be upon arrival – where young children are given choices to settle them in, or on a Friday afternoon as a reward for good work undertaken during the week. Making choices like this may be very difficult for children with autism to do. Again, choices are not 'scripted', and some children with autism may struggle with this. One good way to alleviate this is to provide a 'choosing board'. This would incorporate a few ideas for what the child is able to choose on, say, a Friday afternoon. You could have a photograph or visual of the computer, games, drawing materials, etc. and the child can go to the board for suggestions. I would have the board at the child's height and only display one or two choices, depending on the length of time available to the child.

I would recommend that you use a visual to denote the 'choosing board'. Some symbols are commercially available to help you, one that is common is a depiction of a pointing finger 'choosing' an activity.

'Choosing time' can also be used as a reward for work that is completed well and/or within the timescales that you have set for the child.

Whole school assemblies are often problematic for children with autism for a number of reasons. First, the noise levels of a whole school full of children in a hall can be too much for some children, and they may associate the hall with that noise and perhaps even refuse to enter. In these instances, I would opt for the child to be allowed to wear ear defenders or sit at the back of the hall. When they are sitting at the back, they can see everything, there are no big sudden surprises happening behind them, and no-one is looking at them wearing their ear defenders. Now, before you say but wee Johnny won't be able to see what is going on, well yes, that is true, but if he is sitting slightly to the side at the back of the hall, then he probably would. In general, I would always place the child at the end of an aisle where they would not have to be 'squished' in between other children (they may be hypersensitive to touch), and if they are sitting at the end of the aisle and really *do* want to leave the hall, less of a fuss can be made about it. Again, I would not insist that they remain if they are really not coping with it. You can use the 'first and then' approach to encourage participation, or you can use a sand timer to denote how long assembly will last. A word of caution: if the assembly is to last for, say thirty minutes, then I would suggest that if it does go on for any longer than that, then this could be problematic for the child with autism. They may then expect that future assemblies will also go on for longer than was promised and they may not wish to come along the next time.

Sports day

Sports day is another time when events cannot be scripted to the letter. Now, for most children, this is seen as an exciting event where they have fun and enjoy being outdoors in the fresh air. For some children with autism, however, sports day can be viewed as yet another time for stress for the following reasons:

- Not understanding the purpose of the event – they perhaps do not understand why children have to compete against each other or participate at all – again, this is a *social* event, and it may not be well understood or appreciated by a child with autism

- Children are usually put into teams – this can be difficult for a child with autism, given their social difficulties and sensory needs

- The day itself can be very unpredictable – events can change from moment to moment, as can the weather

- It is a big change to the normal routine – perhaps they are not able to communicate to you that they may prefer to keep things the same, and that they would actually prefer to carry on with their class lessons

- They may struggle with not being able to participate, as they may have difficulty with the physical elements, e.g. they may not have very good co-ordination

- The noise levels may overwhelm them – sports days are, by their very nature noisy events, with lots of children and staff cheering others on to do well

- The large crowds of parents, grandparents and other onlookers watching may be too distracting for them

The key to any successful sports day lies in the planning and preparation of the event. You will know in advance when the day is likely to occur, and so, it would help if you could plan for the event as soon as you know when it is. You can do this in the following ways:

- Crossing off the days on a calendar – *visually* showing them when the event will occur

- Giving as much information as you can about what will happen on the day – what it will actually 'look like', e.g. the layout of the grounds, the equipment and so on

- Practising team sports events during gym lessons so that the games are well rehearsed in advance, and the child with autism knows what is expected of them. You could utilise your child's buddy as their partner – a familiar face helps

- Practising the cheering but tell the child with autism that it is acceptable for them to cover their ears if the noise becomes too loud. They may wish to put in small earphones to nullify the noise

- Practising some of the more difficult co-ordination tasks, but if they are still struggling with this, then perhaps they could take on a different role on the day for that game, e.g. keeping the scores, or directing others on to the next event, i.e. a marshalling role

Everything, really, is about communication and how well you relay information to the child with autism in your class. If you explain things very clearly, and at a pace and level that they understand, then problems should be minimised.

Suggested reading

Social Stories™: http://carolgraysocialstories.com/social-stories/what-is-it/
Comic Strip Conversations: www.autism.org.uk/16261

Chapter Six
BEHAVIOUR MANAGEMENT

As mentioned in Chapter 1, it is often the behaviour of children with autism that will initially raise some eyebrows in class, both from the teacher, and from the other children. This chapter will detail some of the common behaviours that I have witnessed over the years, and the strategies that I have successfully used to alleviate some of these challenges.

If you have already begun to implement some of the strategies previously discussed in this book, then you may find that some of the behaviours I will now discuss may not happen at all, or they may occur less frequently, as a result of your intervention.

Before I discuss, however, how the child with autism may or may not behave in class, I would like you to examine closely how *you* behave in class. Now, this may sound strange, but when you take a close look at some of the ways in which you interact with the children, it may help to shed some light on why the child with autism may not behave in quite the way that you had hoped they would. Here are some questions for you.

- First of all, are you calm? This may sound an odd thing to ask, but I have found over the years that the calmer *you* are, the calmer the *children* are. If you are stressed, you may naturally act differently, and children with autism will notice your face turning redder as you become more anxious, they will notice that slight elevation in the pitch of your voice, perhaps the raised volume, and they will also notice that you may be speaking, and moving, more quickly. All of these changes in your demeanour may have a negative effect on the child with autism who is struggling to process why these changes are happening to you. So when you are very stressed because another child has been misbehaving, and you reprimand them, then wee Johnny may not understand why this has produced a change in *your* behaviour.

- Is the language that you currently use in class suitable for a child with autism to understand? Does the pace, content and volume suit their needs? If not, then maybe *this* is why they are not following your verbal instructions, or worse, are confused and worried about not being able to do so, and they may react inappropriately as a result of this.

- Are you meeting their sensory needs appropriately (there is more on sensory differences in Chapter 8)?

- Are you putting too many demands on them to 'join in'? – I have heard staff previously say to me "well, we live in the real world, and wee Johnny just has to learn to fit in and make friends". As discussed earlier, this won't magically happen overnight. Developing social skills takes time and patience, and speaking of patience...

- Just how patient are you? When working with children with autism, you need to have a great deal of patience, as they may require more support than your typically developing child who does not have autism.

If you are doing everything you can to support wee Johnny, and have lots of patience and a very calm demeanour about you, but he is still not displaying appropriate behaviour in class, then it is important to try to establish *why* he is behaving in this way.

For any child, irrespective of an autism diagnosis, inappropriate behaviours can occur, but all behaviours are present for a reason. It is our job as educators to establish the *function* of the behaviour. Here are some reasons why a *child with autism* may not behave appropriately.

- To have sensory needs met (this can also include hunger, thirst, tiredness, pain, illness). Sensory differences can play a huge part in their daily activities, and if their senses are hyper or hyposensitive, then they may react in ways that are not immediately obvious to someone who does *not* experience such differences.

- To maintain consistency and routines. This is very important for a child with autism, and so they may behave in a way that is unacceptable, in order to maintain that consistency, e.g. throwing themselves to the floor if asked to move on to a new task.

- To attempt to communicate their needs. It may be difficult for them to communicate their needs *verbally*, so other means of gaining your attention may work more quickly for them.

- To attempt to communicate their 'wants.' A child with autism may attempt to take what they want – even if it does not belong to them – this could be due to their difficulties with 'theory of mind' (understanding that another person may be thinking differently to them).

- To attempt to socialise. I have seen many children with autism try to initiate interaction by hitting a child or grabbing a child – unaware that this is socially inappropriate.

- To protest. Some children with autism may find it difficult to communicate why they feel uncomfortable or upset, and so may react *physically*, rather than *verbally*.

- To gain a *predictable* response from another person. If another child or adult has a particular reaction, and the child with autism gains pleasure from this, then the behaviour is likely to be repeated, in order for them to have that same reaction each time.

- Associations made of places, people or objects with previously negative experiences. If, for example, their first encounter with a particular experience was upsetting to them, they may then find it difficult to move on from that memory.

I will now detail some behaviours that are commonly found in *typically developing children*, but it is important to note that the behaviour of children with autism should not be viewed in the same way as their peers as, unlike their peers, they generally *do not* misbehave in order to:

- Annoy others (including you) deliberately

- Cause others to be reprimanded

- Gain social 'kudos' by misbehaving

- Be stubborn (just for the sake of it)

- Be defiant (just for the sake of it)

Behaviour management

Each of these five reasons assumes that the child responsible for the behaviour is *socially motivated* to misbehave, and that these behaviours are *conscious* acts. A child with autism may not have that intrinsic desire to please or displease you or their peers.

Problems can arise, however, when a child with autism is, for example, repeatedly engaging in unwanted behaviours, such as tapping continually on their desk with a pencil. If asked to stop, they continue, and this could be misconstrued as the child demonstrating defiance. Upon closer examination, however, it could be that their sensory needs are being met with the tapping motion. Please take care not to superimpose *your* perception of the situation before exhausting all other possible *autism* based explanations.

So, as you can see, there may be many reasons why some behaviours are happening. So what kind of behaviours are you likely to witness? You may see a child hitting themselves or others. These types of behaviour are the most worrying, for obvious reasons, and yet there is often a simple explanation for their occurrence. When a child with autism is self-injuring, this can be due to a variety of reasons, including pain in the area that they are hitting, being hyposensitive to pain and so hitting themselves can give sensory feedback, frustration at not being understood, or anger if they feel that they have been wronged by someone else.

To ascertain if they are hitting out due to pain, I would ask them if they are sore, and where it hurts. This may sound obvious, but, as mentioned earlier, some children with autism will not instinctively understand that they ought to tell you if they are in pain.

If the behaviour is to gain sensory feedback, then I would offer a sensory alternative; e.g. if they are throwing items around the room to gain visual feedback, I would re-direct this visual stimulation to a more appropriate alternative – throwing bean bags into a bucket, or giving them some time with their sensory box to try to calm them.

If the behaviour is due to frustration at not being understood, then giving suggestions as to what could be upsetting them, or asking their peers if they have witnessed anything that has upset them, might shed some light on their frustrations.

If the behaviour is due to the child with autism feeling upset because of another child's actions, then it is important to speak with both parties to figure out what has gone wrong.

You may see a child with autism hit out at others, a classroom assistant or even you. In such cases, it is important to try to remain calm, as your reaction will either escalate or de-escalate the situation. Again, it is important to try to establish why this has happened, but *not* at the time of the incident – children who are in the middle of such behaviours will take in very little that you say, and so best to avoid any conversation, other than saying their name and an instruction to 'stop!' (using a firm, but not raised voice). Re-directing the child to a quieter area of the classroom such as a pop-up tent or quiet corner of the room, will provide a place for them to calm, and allow for the safety of the other children. It is a good idea to show a visual of the area, rather than use any words at this time. There may be times when a child is having an overwhelming 'moment' and is displaying very physical behaviours towards the other children. In such instances, it is important to remove the *other* children from the situation. Trying to remove the child with autism in these situations can add to the stress that they are already experiencing and will escalate the behaviour further.

A good way to identify when and why behaviours occur is to make a note of any 'triggers'. These could include places, people, events, sensory differences, or perhaps a combination of all of these. There are very good ABC – 'Antecedent', 'Behaviour' and 'Consequences' – charts available for this online.

Strategies that are particularly helpful include:

- Keeping calm and using very little language – this is very important, and I do not apologise for mentioning it frequently. Your whole demeanour is extremely vital in providing consistency and predictability for them.

- Using a countdown (this will vary according to the child's understanding of number, but very useful if they have an interest in numbers). You can vary the countdown, moving down a number scale, according to their motivation level with numbers – you can also do this (if they are very good with numbers) in blocks of ten, e.g. thirty, twenty, ten, zero.

- Using favourite characters as role models, e.g. 'Batman would do this/say this...' – it is important to use positive language e.g. 'Batman would do this/say this', rather than 'Batman wouldn't do that', as this may cause confusion for them. Also remember to keep your language to the minimum required to convey your message.

Behaviour management

- Distraction – by using this strategy, you will 'snap' the child out of their current train of thought, but you have to use it wisely, e.g. suddenly gasping and saying 'oh look at that!' or switching off the lights can sometimes work – this will only be appropriate if the child is *not* having a 'meltdown' and is best achieved at the *beginning* of the behaviour.

- Using a 'first and then' approach – having the 'then' item as a particularly motivating activity for the child. I have used this one on numerous occasions to great effect.

- Reminding the child of the classroom rules – a great deal of children with autism are quite 'rule-driven' – so much so, that they may adopt the 'role' of class police officer to correct others. When this happens, you can simply remind them of the main rule, and that is that *you* are in charge of the children within the classroom. Again, they are doing this as they are taking the rules very literally, and if others are not adhering to them, then they themselves feel a sense of wrongdoing and a need therefore, to correct them. This can lead to their being ostracised for being a 'teacher's pet', not realising the social implications of such behaviour.

- Reward chart – this has to be meaningful for them and you can personalise it with their favourite characters. This can be portable and used as a visual reminder of what they are aiming to achieve.

- Using a 'time out' visual to indicate that *they, or you,* can request that they have some time to think or calm. You can also use an object of reference such as a sand timer.

- Social Stories™ – these can be invaluable in teaching appropriate social skills in an easily understood way – see suggested reading at the end of Chapter 5.

- Comic strip conversations – as with Social Stories™ – can be very useful in addressing social faux pas – see suggested reading at the end of Chapter 5.

- Using humour – this is very much dependent on the child and their understanding and use of humour – some children with autism respond well to humour and can be coaxed into co-operation. Please do not use sarcasm as a means of humour, this is something that children with autism can find very difficult to appreciate or even understand, due to their literal interpretation of language.

- Planned ignoring – if the behaviour is not harming them or another child, but is merely a little annoying for you (like the continual tapping of the pencil on the desk), then you can actively ignore this, especially if it is giving sensory feedback or relief for the child – please remember, they are not doing it to annoy you on purpose.

Here are some typical behaviours that I have witnessed over the years and the strategies that I have successfully used to 'defuse' situations. I have displayed them in the form of a table for quick reference. I have listed a few strategies for each of the behaviours, as what may work for one child, might not for another. Similarly, what may work one day for one child, may not work for them on a subsequent occasion.

Behaviour	Possible reason	Strategies
Running out of class	Overwhelmed by noise	Ear defenders/'concentration station' to work/volume gauge to reduce noise levels/'no entry' sign on inside of door to indicate no entry to outside of the class.
Always wanting to be first in line	Desire for sameness	Establish rota for who is the line leader and display on wall (different child each time children line up).
Refusal to leave outdoor play to return to class	Just enjoying being outside	Use 'first and then' card to indicate first line up then... (something to motivate the return to class). Countdown from 10 – when I say '1' you will be in the line. Reward chart for co-operation with the teacher.
Shouting out the answers	Social skills difficulty	Social story about shouting out in class. Reminder of the class rule about shouting out in class. Child can write down the answer and show it to the teacher at the end to check if they were correct.
Refusal to eat school lunch	Sensory difference –Texture? Taste? Smell?	Give plenty of notice of what is on offer for lunch. Send menu home to parents and ask them to highlight foods that they will eat. Reward chart for eating/trying to eat lunch (three out of five eaten will receive a reward of the child's choosing). Social story about the importance of trying different foods. Packed lunch?

Behaviour management

Behaviour	Possible reason	Strategies
Refusal to wash hands after going to the toilet	Sensory difference – smell of soap? Water too cold/hot?	Visual timetable of hand washing routine displayed at child's height level above sink.
Grabbing at another child's items	Unaware of social nicety of asking permission	Social story on why it is important to ask permission before borrowing items. Modelling the correct way to ask permission. Using the 'concentration station'.
Refusal to leave preferred activity (e.g. computer)	Just enjoying the computer/desire for sameness	Have a timer at the workstation (sand timer works best)/have a 'closed' sign hung over the screen if not in use/have a rota of who can access the computer and for how long/countdown from twenty/'first and then' strategy.
Throws self to the floor when leaving one area of the school to move to another	Dislike of changes/Transitions between events	Use visual timetable to alert the child to what is next on the timetable (giving five minute warning)/'first and then' strategy/countdown/humour/distraction (sudden surprised – not loud – voice to 'snap' child out of the 'moment'.)

There are some times, however, when it is not always possible to establish an obvious reason why a child with autism is not coping. These are the difficult times when, for example, they may exhibit behaviours that are concerning not only to themselves, but to others in class. These behaviours are often called 'meltdowns' for a very good reason. For children with autism who may struggle to communicate their needs or their 'wants', it can often be more productive for them to react vocally, physically or both, to have these needs or 'wants' met. As there may be little understanding of why this is socially unacceptable, then there is no obvious reason for wee Johnny *not* to throw himself to the floor to protest (instinctively), if he is presented with mashed potatoes, instead of the expected French fries, in the dining hall.

So what reasons could lead to such meltdowns? Some of these 'triggers' can include the following:

- Sudden, abrupt changes to routines

- Noise levels

- Heat levels

- Sudden weather changes

- Different teacher in class

- Another child upset/sick/misbehaving/borrowing their items without permission

- If their pencil breaks

- If they do not have the right colour of pen or pencil

- Getting their clothes/hands/face dirty or wet

- Having an accident and tearing their clothes

- Losing or misplacing an item

- Fear or phobia about a particular item (more on this shortly)

- Feeling unwell/tired/thirsty or hungry

- Having a clothing label 'scratching' them

Fears and phobias

One of those reasons was fears and phobias. This is a common occurrence in children with autism, who may present with very exaggerated, and sometimes unusual fears and phobias. I have worked with some children with autism who have had phobias about birthdays, balloons, dogs and fireworks. Having such strong phobias about particular items can be very frightening for children with autism, especially if they are unable, or unaware, that they ought to communicate this fear to you. If you can, for a moment, think of something that would terrify you, and then imagine that you cannot describe to another person exactly how that makes you feel – or worse, you are told that you are being silly to have such a phobia, and that it is not something to be frightened of – then you are some way to understanding why it can be so difficult for a child with autism to cope.

This is one of the many reasons why it is so important to establish a good two-way dialogue with the parents of the child with autism. They are the 'go to' people who have all of this knowledge about what exactly will trigger a 'meltdown', and it may be something that you would not expect – such as seeing an image of their phobia in a film you are watching, or outside of the school grounds. Parents are best placed, also, to tell you which signs the child displays to indicate that a 'meltdown' is imminent. This may involve the child fidgeting excessively, humming to themselves, self-stimulating to gain sensory feedback, tensing their muscles, displaying facial grimacing, flicking their fingers and so on. Each child with autism may have a different way to 'show' that they are experiencing overwhelming feelings that they cannot, or do not, know how to control.

When you see these tell-tale signs in the child with autism in your class, this is the time to acknowledge their anxiety. You can do this very subtly by approaching them (it is important that they see you coming, as suddenly appearing from nowhere may add to their stress). You could try to use the distraction technique of asking them about their favourite topic, this can sometimes 'snap' them out of the intense stress by shifting their attention away from it. If you know what is causing them to have a 'moment', then you could try to prevent that from continuing; for example, if it is caused by their having to do handwriting, then you can use the 'first/then' technique of 'first handwriting, then computer' (or their favourite subject, it may be 'first handwriting, then pop the bubble wrap'). If the cause of the impending 'moment' is another child, then you can ask that child to go on a long message to each of the other classes, or you can ask the child with autism if they would like to go to the 'concentration station' to do their work. It may be, however, that if you have exhausted all of these possibilities, and the child does not appear to be calming, then perhaps they might like to go on a message to get out of the classroom for a short while to alleviate their stress.

Meltdowns

So what does a meltdown look like? It can be very frightening sometimes to witness a child with autism who is really struggling to cope, and who is reacting vocally, physically, or both. Many of the 'moments' I have seen over the years have included lots of physical throwing about of arms and legs, spitting, head-butting, pulling hair, biting, and screaming. I have also witnessed children injure themselves by banging their head with their fist, hitting their head on the desk, door and even against a window. Very often, these types of actions are called 'aggressive' and 'violent', but these words imply that the child with autism is *consciously* seeking to cause harm (once again assuming that they are socially motivated to injure others), when in fact, they are simply *reacting* in a way that is not socially acceptable to someone who is not directly experiencing what they are going through. So, I prefer to call these behaviours 'reactive', rather than 'aggressive' or 'violent'.

When a child is, as I refer to it, 'having a moment', it is best to use as little language as possible, as they might not be able to register what you are saying, as their senses are already overloaded.

If they, or another child, is in danger of being hurt, then it is best to remove the other children quietly from the scene – ask one of your other pupils to fetch an adult to do this – a laminated piece of red coloured paper with an exclamation mark to show to the adult, is a good visual cue for them to come quickly.

When the other children are out of the class, the noise level will immediately drop, and so this will aid the child with autism's ability to calm much more quickly. Sometimes, this is just enough to de-escalate the situation and bring them down to a calmer state of mind. I find it helps too, if you can dim, or if this is not possible, turn off the lights. This also helps, I feel, to 're-boot' the child, and I mean this in a kind way, as the extra sensory stimulation can be just too overwhelming for them.

It is important to remember that you are trying to help the child with autism, and so you should avoid reacting, as you perhaps would to a child who is having a tantrum – this is most certainly *not* a tantrum, as tantrums are *conscious* acts that seek to manipulate others to achieve an end product – the child with autism having a 'meltdown' is simply overwhelmed and is not consciously trying to profit from it.

Parents may have their own tried and tested strategies for managing their child's 'meltdowns' at home and, if these work well, then you should use them too, where possible.

Behaviour management

Some useful strategies for de-escalating the situation can include:

- Avoid giving direct eye contact with the child – looking directly into the child's eyes can add to the sensory overload. It would help if you could sit near to, but not directly beside them, preferably at their side (from a small distance)

- Use little or no language, but it is important that if you have to speak to them, that you keep your volume low, speak slowly, and use positive language

- Avoid talking about what is happening to them, as they will not be able to process what you are saying

- Do not criticise or chastise them – they are not in control of themselves at this point

- Wait patiently until you can see that they are showing signs of calming

- It can help to show a visual of a calm image that they can present to you to indicate that they are calm and ready to move on (these are readily available online – see suggested reading at the end of this chapter)

'Moments' can last for just a few minutes, but 'meltdowns' can last for some time, and so it's best not to 'rush' a child with autism 'out of it', as this can only prolong it. I have previously made the mistake of assuming that the child with autism was calm and ready to carry on with what they were doing beforehand, but when I spoke to the child they clearly were not ready to, and this triggered another 'moment'.

It is so important not to discuss the incident with the child when they are coming out of it. They may not be aware of why it has happened, so do not question them about it or even comment on it. It is best just to move on to the next item on their visual timetable, but if you know that the next item is something that they are not keen to do, then give them a choice of another task that you know they would like.

Some people may think that you are rewarding their 'meltdown' by giving them choices, but this is not the case. You are recognising that they have been very distressed and overwhelmed, and you are acknowledging and rewarding the calm state of mind that they are now displaying.

Other children in your class may not know that the child has autism; the child with autism may not even know themselves. It is not your job to tell the class, as you would be divulging information about a child's medical condition, and, in so doing, you could run the risk of litigation should that confidential information be disclosed to others. Do not be tempted to explain why wee Johnny is having a 'moment'; it is sufficient to say to the children that everyone deals with situations in a different way, and that they can help by carrying on as normal. You may have one or two children in your class who may try to copy some of the behaviours that they see in wee Johnny, and that is when you can utilise the behaviour management skills that you would normally deploy for a child who does *not* have autism. This can be very tricky for you, especially when the tough questions come up, such as 'well *he* was shouting out', or '*he* was hitting others'. My response to those types of questions would always be that 'we are talking about *your* behaviour right now'. Some parents of children with autism may feel that it is appropriate to tell the children in class about their child's diagnosis, and if they do, it would be best not to have the child there to hear everyone talking about them; all of this attention on them could be upsetting to them. This is very much a parental decision, and should be left entirely up to parents to decide if this is appropriate for them, and for their child.

Suggested reading

Theory of Mind:
www.educateautism.com/infographics/sally-anne-test.html
Boardmaker™: www.mayer-johnson.com/boardmaker-software/

Chapter Seven
EDUCATIONAL TRIPS

Going on a trip or educational visit, is an occasion that most children will anticipate with eager enthusiasm. For some children with autism, however, this can be a very challenging time, and can cause them to become quite distressed, even at the very mention of it. So why could this be? Let's look at some of the possible reasons:

- Trips involve changes to their everyday routines

- Perhaps the child has not been to this place before, and is anxious about what to expect there

- Perhaps the mode of transport to get them there is one that they are not familiar with using, or is a type of transport in which they do not like to travel

- The unstructured nature of the visit, as opposed to the very structured nature of everyday class work

- The length of the journey

- The close proximity when sitting next to their peers throughout the journey

- Having lunch in a different location

- The unpredictability of the day's events

- Sudden changes to the weather (if the trip is largely outdoors)

- Not knowing what is expected of them and perhaps not understanding the purpose of their visit

- Anxious about when the visit will end – will it go on forever?

- Not having as many opportunities to sit down and rest – some children with autism can get very tired very quickly

- Meeting different people on the visit and having to interact with them

- Anxious about toileting in an unfamiliar location

These are just some of the possible reasons why a child with autism may struggle to enjoy that lovely trip you and your pupils, are excited about.

So, what can you do to try to alleviate all of these concerns? Well, the key to organising any successful trip, be it near or far, is in the planning and preparation. I cannot stress enough how important it is to be as organised as you can, and to plan for any events that may occur. At the end of this chapter is a helpful checklist to assist you with this planning. Obviously, you will be following your school's guidance on planning trips, and I will not insult your intelligence by telling you how to plan a trip, but, for a child with autism, there will need to be quite a few adaptations that I would suggest you make in order to give them a really worthwhile and enjoyable experience that they will remember, for all the right reasons.

First and foremost, I would discuss the trip with the child's parents. They are best placed to advise you on how their child copes on such outings, and any pitfalls that you may encounter. They will also be an invaluable source of information regarding particular strategies that they have successfully used on previous occasions.

Let's now look at how you can help the child with autism in your class to enjoy their trip.

Planning the trip

Let's use as an example a day visit to, say, a farm. Many children are brought up in towns and cities with little experience of going out into the countryside, let alone to visit a farm, so that would be a good example to use.

First thing you should try to do is to visit the farm yourself – I feel that this is quite important for the following reasons:

- It would give you an opportunity to see the facilities: where the children can have their packed lunch, or what food they can purchase if they are not taking their lunch, and whether they cater for specific dietary preferences.

- How many toilets there are, and where they are located?

- Are there indoor facilities, should the weather take a turn for the worse?

- Is there a 'quiet zone' that the child with autism can retreat to should they be over-whelmed on the trip? (this could possibly include the option of going back to the coach with a member of staff, if the coach is to remain at the venue).

- You will be able to gain a *sensory* picture of what is on offer, are the odours too strong? Will this bother the child with autism in your class who may be hypersensitive to smells?

- What can they actually *do* there? Will there be lots of 'dead' times where the children are just to listen to someone talking about the farm? Times like these can seem pointless to some children with autism.

- Are there opportunities for the children to run around safely to let off steam?

- Are there play facilities?

- Is there a shop for them to purchase items?

One of the most important reasons to visit, is that it affords you an opportunity to take lots of photographs of the places and the people that the child with autism in your class is likely to encounter.

Having gained a picture of what the visit will 'look like', and if you are entirely happy with everything, then it's time to think about the journey.

Making travel arrangements

Most visits by schools nowadays involve travelling by coach. If you are very familiar with the coach company and have used them before, it would help if you could speak to them, and ask them a few questions too, including information about:

- Times when the coach will arrive at the school and leave the venue

- If the coach will be staying at the venue, or if the driver will leave and return later

- You could also request that music be played, or not, (as appropriate) during the journey. Some pupils with autism like listening to music and it could be a good distraction to the changes to their routine, but for others, this may add to their anxiety, particularly if they are hypersensitive to sounds

- If there are toileting facilities on the coach

Discussing the trip with the class

Having planned the venue and the transport, it is now time to talk about the proposed trip with the child with autism (and the rest of the class!). I would introduce the idea with much excitement and enthusiasm – if you appear stressed talking about it to a child with autism, they may pick up on the changes to your tone of voice and demeanour, and then make negative associations with the idea of going on the trip.

You could then show the children the photographs that you've taken of the venue and explain what you will be doing there, and all of the interesting things that they might see. This will help to give some structure and predictability to the visit for the child with autism.

Having explained where they will be going and the purpose of the visit, you could then introduce a large calendar to the class. This will be a visual countdown to the proposed visit, and the children can take turns to cross off each day to signify *visually*, when the trip will occur. I would give at least four weeks' preparation time, this gives the child with autism time to acclimatise to the notion of going on the visit, but is not too long a time frame that they will lose interest.

It would also help if you could put some information in the child's home/school diary about any special equipment or clothing that the child is likely to require for the trip.

This may include a change of footwear or jacket and, for some children, this in itself could be problematic, so advance notice of this is vital.

A week before the trip, I would go through the checklist that I have included for you at the end of this chapter. This will ensure that you have not forgotten anything that might make the trip a bit more successful for the child with autism.

The day before the trip, I would let the class know about the arrangements in terms of supervision; placing the children into groups. I have been on lots of school visits where parents and staff from other areas of the school have been asked to come along to keep the pupil/adult ratios at a legal level. I would recommend that the child with autism in your class go in *your* group. This gives the child a familiar face and will minimise the stress of having a 'stranger' as their group leader.

Trip day

On the day of the trip, you may witness some unexpected behaviour that might be inappropriate. This may be due to the fact that the child with autism might be very nervous about the event, and so it is very important that *you* remain calm and in control of the situation – this will help to alleviate some of the stress that they may be experiencing.

When the class is seated, I would go through a visual plan of what the day will look like, beginning as follows:

- Photograph of coach – brief explanation of where the children will sit (I would let wee Johnny go first in the line today, so that he can choose which seat he would like on the coach – this is not the time for debating the line leader issue)
- Clock – to indicate how long the journey will last
- Photograph of the venue sign to indicate where you are going
- Usual visual to indicate lunch – I would give an approximate timing for lunch, e.g. 12.30–1.30. If you are *too* prescriptive with a definite time, and something untoward happens to deviate from that time, then it could be problematic for the child with autism, and subsequently for you also
- Photograph of some of the events/animals you may see
- Photograph of the coach (to indicate that it is time to leave)
- Photograph of the school (to indicate that you will be returning to the school – don't assume that they will know that they'll be coming back from the trip)

All of these photographs should have no more than a single sentence to describe them, e.g. 'First, we get on the coach'. Using too much language will only 'muddle' things.

It may help you in the long run, if you do a smaller version for the child – your classroom assistant, if you have this luxury, could prepare this by laminating the photographs and attaching them to a key ring that the child can refer to on the day.

As mentioned earlier, giving approximate timings for the day's events can be very helpful in indicating when events are expected to occur – this would certainly give the child with autism much more predictability to the day.

During the coach ride, the child with autism may feel anxious about the whole event, and so I would suggest that they have a window seat, so that they can be distracted by events going on outside, rather than having to engage in 'chit-chat' that they may feel will only add to their growing stress levels. You can also ask the child whom they would like to sit beside – I would give two options, as more than this may confuse them, or cause them to become even more stressed (you could include yourself as an option).

If it helps to have music playing through headphones, then this should be allowed. You are not giving special privileges to the child with autism, but rather, you are showing true inclusion of their disability by meeting their needs, rather than having the child with autism 'fit into' what everyone else is doing. If you think about, if the child with autism had a physical disability that warranted the need for a walking stick, you would not take away the stick because other children did not have one, would you, so why should you take away the items that they may need for their disability – albeit a largely *invisible* disability.

I would keep a very close eye on the child with autism throughout the trip for signs that they may not be coping – some of those signs were discussed in Chapter 6. Look out for the individual signals that they are giving you to indicate rising tension, and act calmly and quickly to defuse this, by using some of the strategies discussed earlier.

If you sense that the whole experience is becoming a bit overwhelming for them, and they do not appear to be enjoying it, then you could try to incorporate some of their interests to give them a bit of comfort. If they enjoy technology, then perhaps they could be the official photographer on the day to take photographs of the places and people that they meet? This could then be put into a scrapbook, as part of a future literacy lesson. This would also be beneficial to them, as it would keep them *positively* occupied, and thus possibly take their thoughts away from feeling anxious. It would also be an opportunity for them to socialise with their peers when asking them if they would like to have their photograph taken (you may need to model how they could ask this).

Educational trips

You could also give them a clipboard and ask them to cross off each animal that they see, and depending on their level of ability, you could write down some questions that they will need to answer (multiple choice of three should make this less stressful).

Throughout the trip, I would give a 'five minutes until' warning for each new event. This will give them time to accept the new event; it may be lunch or seeing the lambs, but whatever the event, giving that time to process what is coming next, is very helpful to a child with autism, and should not be underestimated.

The 'five minutes until' warning should always be given just before the end of the trip, and I would accompany this verbal warning with a visual of the coach, and then a visual of the school. The child with autism may, however, have no desire whatsoever to return to the coach, or the school for that matter, as they have been enjoying themselves tremendously, and the strategies I would deploy for such occasions would be as follows:

- Using the countdown strategy – this can be as simple as 'Johnny, on the coach when I get to zero...ten, nine...'

- You can also use the tried and tested 'You are going to be first on the coach – this will make you the winner!'

- The 'first and then' strategy also works well here – 'first coach, then music' (or whatever will motivate them). You can ask parents for a special treat to entice them back on the coach – this can be produced as a 'then' item to motivate them to comply (this could be a comic, favourite toy or sensory item). I would remind you again that you have to follow this through, as failure to deliver what you promised, will only result in the child with autism forming a great sense of mistrust in you

Once back on the coach, I would give an estimated time of arrival back at the school – given traffic and weather conditions etc. About five minutes before arrival, I would give a verbal 'five minutes until', to indicate this. Use the time on the coach to write in their home/school diary how they coped with the day's events – again, try to highlight the positive elements. You can write down a few things that they would have seen on the trip, just in case they do not wish to recall the day's events – some children with autism may feel that this is a pretty pointless exercise for them (again, it is a social 'nicety' to tell your loved ones about the fabulous day you had.)

Back at school, the child with autism may not wish to exit the coach. Again, you can use the strategies you successfully deployed to get them *onto* the coach.

When you arrive back at school, you can remind the child with autism that tomorrow (assuming it is not a Friday) is a 'school day', as normal. If it is a Friday, remind them that tomorrow will be a 'home day' with no school.

Checklist for Day Trip Visit

Action	Completed (tick for 'yes')	Comments
Visit location		
Take photographs of the following items (this can be done on a visit or taking a 'screenshot' of the website).		
Venue sign/logo		
Dining facilities		
Wet weather facilities		
Appropriate personnel (with their permission)		
Ask about the following (this can be done if you make a visit yourself or discuss over the telephone)		
Toileting facilities		
Areas to 'let off steam'?		
Areas to 'chill out'?		
Wet weather facilities		
Shop for purchasing souvenirs?		
Special clothing to be worn, e.g. wellington boots?		

Residential trips

Trips that involve the child living in a different environment that they are used to for any period of time, require very careful thought and planning, and can be problematic for children with autism. Let's look at why this might be so. Living away from home involves changes to the following:

- Everyday routines – not being in school, but with teacher and peers out of the usual environment

- Being away from family and familiar faces. Unpredictability about what will happen/when it will happen/how long the trip will last

- Eating habits – not eating the same food as at home, not eating dinner with the same people, different dining area, perhaps eating at a different time, different crockery and cutlery

- Sleeping arrangements – sharing a room with peers rather than with siblings, or by themselves, having a different bed, duvet and pillow. Noises from peers who are sharing the room, different smells. Lights out at perhaps an earlier time. Difficulty with getting to sleep

- Unfamiliarity of the general environment

So, as you can imagine, it may be quite stressful for a child with autism to cope with all of that, especially if the trip involves foreign travel.

Now that we've established why this would be difficult for a child with autism, we can look at some ways that you can help to minimise this anxiety and give the child a positive and enjoyable experience that they will remember fondly.

As with the day trip, I would first have a meeting with the parents to have a discussion around possible difficulties that their child may face on the trip. If the child has any medication to take whilst they are on the visit, this would need to be discussed also. I have prepared a handy questionnaire that may help with your parents' meeting at the end of this chapter.

As well as meeting with parents, I would advise that early on, you research as much as you can about the accommodation in which you will be residing. Important questions to ask could include the following:

Sleeping facilities

- How many to a room?

- Are there single beds or bunk beds?

- Is there a 'lights out' time?

- Can they accommodate a night light?

- Where is the toilet located in relation to the room? – are there en-suite facilities?

Dining facilities

- Are there set meal times?

- Can they accommodate dietary preferences (some children with autism may have quite specific dietary preferences, or they may be intolerant to gluten or casein)?

- Can the child with autism bring their own crockery and cutlery (if this is an issue for the child and would cause them to become upset)?

Medical/medication facilities

- Where is the nearest hospital (some children with autism may be epileptic, or may have allergies that could result in anaphylactic shock)?

- Where can medication safely be stored?

Staffing

- How will the children be grouped?

- Will the children have the same group leader throughout?

Preparing the child with autism for the trip

If you are happy with all of the above, and the trip planning begins, then it is important to discuss the trip very early on with the child with autism so that you can give as much preparation time as possible – I would only do this after you have met with their parents.

If your trip will involve a long journey, then I would begin by showing the destination on a map – 'Google Earth' is a good resource to display this very clearly and may interest them more than a road map would. It is important to familiarise the child with the destination before you begin to talk about when you are going. If you have been able to take photographs of the location, then this would be great – any visual information will 'cement' the destination. There may be a website of the venue that the children in your class can access, to gain further information about the facilities on offer.

If the child with autism is very motivated by mathematics, then perhaps they could measure the distance to and from the destination, and plot different ways to access the venue.

Now that the child with autism knows *where* they will be visiting, it is important to establish with them *when* they will be going and for how long.

How much notice you will be able to give will largely depend on your school's policies and procedures for organising trips. In my experience, however, for a residential trip, you can expect to know about six months in advance. This will give ample time to acclimatise the child with autism to the idea.

Using a calendar, one displaying the whole year on one page, is a good way to denote the time passing until the trip, without 'flipping' on to the next month. I would suggest that the day of the trip is highlighted in some way, and every day leading up to then could be crossed off at the end of each school day, to signify the time drawing nearer. It would help if the duration of the trip were highlighted or shaded in a different colour.

I would talk regularly about the trip and do so with a happy demeanour; having a worried look on your face may give them cause to be alarmed. I would talk about the length of time they will be away from home, and the sleeping arrangements – it is important to discuss this early on, as they may be worried about this. If you know that they will be sharing a room, perhaps you could ask them if there is a particular child with whom they would like to share? If the child would be more comfortable with their own duvet and pillow, then perhaps the parents could arrange for the child to have these available for the trip? This would certainly give a sense of familiarity. If they are used to having a night light on, then perhaps a hand-held light would suffice instead? Or perhaps you could leave the light outside the room on and the door slightly ajar? You could also discuss (with the other children too) what the dining facilities will look like, what the rules will be, etc.

About a month before the trip, I would start to get practical. I would give the child with autism a list of items that they may need for the journey – this could include a favourite book or toy/iPad/iPod etc. (an iPod would be a good way to mask the excitable noises that their peers may make). You could also add in perhaps some snacks that they would enjoy. As with the day trip, it would helpful to discuss the best seating position for them during travel – again, they may wish to sit next to you to have a familiar face, and for reassurance.

In the time leading up to the trip, I would also discuss what the class would be doing there. You could detail any activities that may be involved, and any other places that you may visit whilst there.

About two weeks before the trip, I would write in the diary to parents to ascertain if anything has changed since the initial meeting – medication/allergies/changes to routines/no longer requires a night light etc. Some children with autism can change preferences for certain items quite quickly – a fascination for Spiderman can quickly change to something else and is no longer a motivation. It is best to keep up to date.

A few days before the trip, I would speak to the child with autism and ask how they are feeling about the trip. This is a good opportunity to gauge if there is something that is worrying them – it might seem to be something simple to someone else but may be causing real anxiety to them.

The day before the trip, I would refer to the calendar again, and remind all of the children of the time that they will be leaving the next day.

Trip day

On the day itself, I would discourage parents from extended goodbyes – this can prolong the anxiety for a child with autism. It's helpful to board the transport as quickly as possible.

Travelling for long distances can be difficult for a child with autism, so keeping them occupied is important. Some children may have small, portable DVD players, or there may be one on the transport you are using – this would help to keep the anxiety level down throughout the journey. Perhaps they could look out for familiar landmarks during the journey and note these down with the timings? Some children with autism can be interested in road signs and motorway junction numbers – perhaps they can also note these down with the timings?

When you get to your destination, I would spend some time familiarising the child with autism with their new 'home' – but I would avoid using these specific words, as they could take what you are saying very literally and be concerned that they will not actually return to their *own* home at the end of the trip.

Perhaps they could take some photographs of the new surroundings? I would also encourage all of the children to create a diary or scrapbook detailing each day of the trip and what they did or saw. This is especially helpful for a child with autism, as they can often need guidance on how to pass the 'downtime' meaningfully. Please don't insist that they join in with social events if they don't wish to do so – they will have enough stress coping with the new surroundings and changes to their routines without having to mingle.

It is important to ensure that the child is comfortable with their new surroundings and with the changes to their routines. You can help with this by having familiar visuals to denote events, e.g. lunch visual, photo of the hotel to indicate when you are returning there after a day's events, photo of the bedroom to indicate bedtime etc.

Another way to bring predictability and familiarity to the child with autism is to encourage them to use their interests whilst you are out and about each day. For example, if they have a specific interest in nature, then you could ask them to note down the different animals that they see.

It's not only important to give preparation for the trip beginning, it is also important to give plenty of notice of when the trip is coming to an end. Some children may be enjoying themselves and not wish for it to end, so this can be quite tricky for them to accept. I would use a calendar to indicate visually when they will be returning to home, and say this (where appropriate to the needs of the particular child), e.g. 'three more days' etc. Some children are very interested in dates and times, so use this if it helps them.

The most important thing to remember is that the whole experience should be fun for everyone – including the child with autism. If you give as much notice and predictability as you can, and if you are aware of their emotional state, and can act upon this to help them, then the trip should be a pleasant one for *all* concerned.

Parents' Questionnaire

What would make the journey a pleasant one, for your child?

....

....

....

Will your child require any medication on the trip? Yes/No

If yes, please give details:

....

....

....

Will your child be comfortable with sharing a room with .... amount of peers?

....

....

....

Does your child require a night light? Yes/No

Will your child be comfortable sleeping in a different bed? Yes/No

If no: Would it help to bring their duvet cover and pillowslip on the trip? Yes/No

If no: Do you have any other suggestions to ensure your child's comfort?

....

....

....

What does your child like to eat?

Breakfast:

....

....

....

Lunch:

....

....

....

Dinner:

....

....

....

Does your child have any fears or phobias? Yes/No

If yes, details:

....

....

....

Do you have any concerns about the trip?

....

....

....

Suggested reading

www.autism.org.uk/professionals/teachers/theatre-and-museum.aspx

Chapter eight
ALL THINGS SENSORY

Using our senses is an unconscious action that most of us take for granted, and we only ever spend time considering them when something upsets the equilibrium. I know this to be true when I am confronted with blaring music from the car next to me at traffic lights, or the high-pitched whine coming from the dentist's drill. If you can imagine, for a moment, what would challenge your senses, and then try to picture this happening on a consistent basis, day in, day out, then you would be in a better position to put yourself in the shoes of a child with autism who has difficulty in interpreting or modulating their senses.

When I speak of the senses, I don't just mean the five senses that we all know, but the other two senses that perhaps you may not know: the vestibular sense (concerned with our balance) and proprioception (the sense that tells us our body position in space). So, in total, there are seven senses that will be discussed within this chapter: visual, auditory, tactile, gustatory (taste), olfactory (smell), vestibular and proprioception.

Many children with autism may exhibit heightened responses from their senses and these responses can, in turn, lead to anxiety, fear, nausea, upset and physical pain. What is quite striking though, is that where we have learned to cope with and rationalise our senses being bombarded or challenged, children with autism may find this difficult to do.

Our job as educators, is to provide a safe, stimulating and enriching environment that is conducive to learning. But often, due to their sensory differences, children with autism, in these very stimulating classroom environments, can find this difficult, and may positively struggle to interpret their senses, make sense of them or, in the worst-case scenario, experience a sensory 'meltdown' (very often mistaken, incorrectly, for a 'tantrum').

One of the most practical things you can do, is to provide a sensory box for the child with autism in your class. This would be as big, or as little as appropriate for the age and stage of the child. I would have their picture on it (or name if this is more age appropriate), and I would ask the child to decorate it with their favourite characters or pictures of items that they enjoy. Inside, I would have items that you know they will enjoy, and that will give them the sensory feedback that they are seeking, examples could include the following:

- 'Chewy tube' for biting (I have previously used this as a good substitute for another child's arm)
- Mini lava lamp
- Fidget toys
- 'Koosh' (squeezy) ball
- Different pieces of textured materials – this is dependent on what the child likes – some may like soft fur, others may like rougher textures
- Light-up toys
- Spinning toys

You could timetable the sensory box into their daily programme or use it as a motivator to engage the child, using the 'first and then' approach discussed earlier – I have used this to great effect. You could also use it as a distraction if you suspect that the child may be approaching a sensory 'meltdown', by intervening prior to that occurring.

So how can you tell when this would be likely to happen? The clues are in the behaviours that they exhibit when their senses are challenged, and this largely depends on whether they are seeking to *stimulate* their senses or are reacting to their senses being stimulated. This is referred to as being hyposensitive or hypersensitive.

Hypersensitive or hyposensitive?

You will often have heard of someone who is described as being 'hyper' – meaning excessive, but usually in terms of energy or enthusiasm. This term can be used to describe how we interpret sensory signals, so, for example, someone can be described as being hypersensitive to sounds (that would be me with the blaring music). This can also be referred to as 'high sensitivity'.

Hyposensitive, on the other hand, is maybe not so commonly used, and describes the opposite to hypersensitivity. This is also called 'low sensitivity'. So, using the same example, someone who is hyposensitive to sounds would really enjoy that blaring music, and would press their ear right up against it, to gain sensory feedback.

It is important that you establish early on if the child with autism in your class has any hyper or hyposensitivites and, again, the best people to ask are the parents. It may be helpful to have them fill in a questionnaire at the start of the session to determine this, but I find that all that form completion is time consuming for parents and so I would suggest a wee chat about it. You can make notes and apply the strategies that I am now going to suggest to you. Sometimes, an Occupational Therapist will undertake a 'sensory profile', and this also determines their sensory needs in terms of hyper and hyposensitivity.

Behaviours associated with sensory differences

It would probably help if I described some typical behaviours that you may witness for each of the senses, and whether this could be as a result of hyper or hyposensitivity, and what you can do to help.

Let me stress here again that each child with autism is different, and so are the sensory requirements for each child. There is no 'magic wand' to fix sensory differences, they are unique to the child; whilst it is helpful to understand why they are behaving or acting in a specific way, it is not necessary always to 'fix' the 'problem' – it may not seem to be a problem to them, and if it is not inappropriate, or causing harm to anyone else, then you should judge whether it really is just bothering *you*, and if so, then I would not try to change it.

The strategies that I am suggesting could be used to help the child with autism to meet their sensory needs in the most *appropriate* way in class. These strategies are not suggested, however, in order for the child with autism to 'fit in' with the rest of the class. There may be some other children in your class who also have sensory needs, but they may have instinctively learned to suppress these (in order to 'fit in'). A child with autism would have difficulty inhibiting their senses in this way.

So, let's look now at some sensory related behaviours you may see, and what action you can take to help. Each of the seven senses is now listed in tables as follows:

Visual

Behaviour	Hypo	Hyper	Action you can take to help
Covering eyes		✓	Seat child with back to bright light/allow child to wear sunglasses in class/copy work on to grey paper (white may be too bright)/have dimmer switch in class or turn off lights if they are not absolutely necessary/tilt blinds to shade area in which they are working.
Plays with reflective, spinning objects, gazes up at lights frequently	✓		Build some time into their schedule to allow for this, say a five-minute slot before break time to indulge in this sensory seeking activity.
Distracted by wall displays and not focusing on work		✓	Where possible, reduce your wall display/move the child to a less 'busy' part of the classroom/use the 'concentration station'.
Flicking pencil or ruler back and forth directly in front of line of vision or to the side using peripheral vision	✓		Use the 'first and then' approach – 'first' this, then five minutes of pencil flicking'/distraction/countdown strategy – using a visual sand timer will give a similar visual stimulation, but will take the focus away from the pencil flicking and will visually remind the child of when the task should be completed.

Auditory

Behaviour	Hypo	Hyper	Action you can take to help
Talking very loudly/shouting/making loud, sudden noises (This behaviour may be an attempt to mask the loud sounds they hear)		✓	Offer earplugs to the child to dampen the noise level/move to a quieter corner of the classroom/move to the 'concentration station'/give small sensory snacks to chew on (chewing can help to nullify the noise level).
Sudden, startled behaviours/screaming		✓	As above, but avoid approaching the child from behind - best to give visual warning of your and other children's approaches. If the noises are coming from chair legs on a hard floor, place felt pads on the legs to minimise the noise/give as much warning as you can for fire drills – visual warning would help and ask them to cover their ears to prepare. Use the volume gauge to audit classroom noise.
Not responding to verbal requests	✓		Write down instructions/use symbols to indicate task requirements/ask child what they have to do – don't assume that if they repeat what you have asked, that they then understand it – it may just be echolalia.
Turns the volume up or plays instruments/sings very loudly.	✓		Use the volume gauge to indicate acceptable noise levels in class.

Tactile

Behaviour	Hypo	Hyper	Action you can take to help
Reacting inappropriately to slightest touch of peer, e.g. hitting out at someone who brushes past them.		✓	Give alternative strategy to child for coping with this, e.g. instead of hitting child, count to ten slowly/social story on how to respond in such situations/ de-sensitising the child to pain when touched through physical contact with peers, e.g. in team games or through role play.
'Drumming' with hands or feet.	✓		Use 'Theraband' – strong, flexible material that wraps around the legs of the chair so that the child can 'push' against it to gain sensory feedback/ fidget spinner/ 'koosh' ball/'therapy putty' – malleable putty that is available in different strengths to improve muscle tone in the hands/raised foot rest – this may be more comfortable and give a sense of 'place' for their feet.
Self-stimulating – these behaviours are often concerned around the mouth area, e.g. biting, spitting, blowing bubbles.	✓		I would always offer a more appropriate replacement, e.g. for biting, I would offer a 'chewy tube' or 'chewelry' – widely available on the internet. For spitting, I would do a Social Story. Blowing bubbles – again, a social story would be appropriate for this, although as long as it doesn't harm anyone, I would overlook this.
Pulling at clothes/ scratching continually		✓	Ask parents if they would mind removing clothing labels – this can often be very uncomfortable for a child who is hypersensitive to touch.

Gustatory

Behaviour	Hypo	Hyper	Action you can take to help
Eats inedible items, e.g. crayons, soil, sand.	✓		Sorting activity to distinguish between edible and non-edible items/offer an alternative that will give the same sensation, e.g. substitute a hard crayon for a hard 'chewy tube'/provide a snack box or oral motor sensory box – (a big picture with an open mouth on the box would denote its purpose) in which you can place all the acceptable substitutes.
Self-restricted diet, only eating 'yellow' foods such as bread, pasta and biscuits.		✓	Have food tasting if you can - never insist on the child with autism trying new foods, even if they have a lick, that would be a good start. Use the 'Batman loves to eat...' (or preferred superhero...)/ have a food trying reward chart – but be realistic, they may only wish to try one new food, and that should be rewarded.
Overfilling their mouth and eating too quickly.	✓		This is a tricky one. If you think that the child is at risk of choking, then you can suggest that they eat more slowly by using a Social Story. You could set a timer for an appropriate time that they need to take to eat their meal (with parents' permission), and that they should not be finished before the allocated time period. Best to supervise children who are at risk of choking for health and safety reasons.
Gagging when others are eating beside them.		✓	Move the child to an area where they are not beside the cause of the gagging (this would most probably be from the smells of others' food but could also be from the taste of their own food. If you move them to a different area and they are still gagging, then it is most probably from what they are eating – speak to parents about alternatives.

Olfactory

Behaviour	Hypo	Hyper	Action you can take to help
Smells objects or people inappropriately	✓		Give the child with autism a handkerchief with essential oils (check with parents to get permission) – this might give the scented feedback they are seeking, and is an unobtrusive way to do so/Social Story about why it makes people upset if someone sniffs them.
Reacts negatively to new smells, e.g. screams/shouts out/hits out.		✓	Give exposure to strong smells gradually in activities, e.g. scented play dough, scent guessing games (have different scents available that are disguised in order that children can match the items to which the scent relates. Change your perfume if it offends their sense of smell (it has happened to me more than once, don't take it personally).

Vestibular

Behaviour	Hypo	Hyper	Action you can take to help
Trips up frequently/clumsy		✓	Ensure your class is clutter free and that there are clear pathways and no obstacles to negotiate/encourage walking rather than running.
Spins around/jumps/climbs onto furniture	✓		Allocate a five minute run around the gym hall with a classroom assistant before class commences/give regular breaks in their schedule to move around/'Theraband' on chair legs/'Move n sit' cushion (cushion with raised 'bumps' to give sensory feedback)/Social story about keeping safe in class (for climbers).

Holding on to walls, chairs when navigating their way around the classroom and school environment.		✓	Ensure clutter free environment as mentioned earlier. Place coloured tape on floor to denote specific areas, e.g. story corner, cloakroom area/mention to parents – you may wish to consider Occupational Therapy input to aid with this.
Throwing items around in class.	✓		I would substitute the throwing of items by having a designated 'throwing area' (I would have a bucket and bean bags to fit this purpose) and timetable this in to their daily schedule (once in morning and once in afternoon) – you can decrease or increase the time as appropriate.

Proprioception

Behaviour	Hypo	Hyper	Action you can take to help
Unaware of own strength - grabbing items or people with a lot of force	✓		Using 'Therapy putty' or 'Koosh' ball to give feedback. Using a visual gauge to indicate too much force – you can demonstrate differing amounts of force using plasticine/Social Story about how it feels for others to be grabbed with force.
Easily fatigued/yawning frequently		✓	Break tasks into smaller 'chunks' to avoid an overwhelming feeling of being overloaded/schedule time for their sensory box (best in the afternoon when they are most in need of a 'chill out' time.

The sensory factor should always be placed high on the agenda of importance when working with children with autism – I cannot emphasise this enough.

There may be occasions when the child with autism in your class is displaying a behaviour that will challenge *your* senses. It is important to understand the *function* of the sensory behaviour – it may be that it is to stimulate their senses to gain sensory feedback, or it may be as a reaction to having their senses stimulated. Once you establish the function, then it is easier to find a solution, rather than compound their distress by becoming stressed yourself.

If the senses are well managed, then the levels of inappropriate behaviours should diminish.

Suggested reading

www.autism.org.uk/sensory

Chapter nine
SOME FINAL THOUGHTS

The fact that you have taken the time to read this book, indicates to me that you are the best person to teach the child with autism in your class, as you have demonstrated a commitment to understanding their difficulties and, therefore, a desire to help them.

Hopefully this book will have given you some insight into how it would feel for wee Johnny to come into a busy environment and navigate his way through the minefields of language, emotions, sensory challenges and social rules and regulations that typically occur within every primary classroom.

I hope that you will now have a better understanding of how best to support any child with autism in your class.

A final word of advice is to foster good relationships with the parents – they may appear to be very defensive of their child but, trust me, they just want the best for their child. They want someone like you to take cognisance of their child's difficulties, and not dismiss their child as just being badly behaved. All too often, parents have had to be defensive when others do not understand their child's difficulties: you cannot 'see' the autism, unlike other conditions where you may *physically* see that the child has a difficulty. If you work *with* parents, you will reap the rewards in terms of helpful information, and the children will ultimately benefit too.

Please think of it like this: it's not about changing a child with autism to fit our environment, but rather, it's about changing our environment to fit a child with autism – that's true inclusion.

Thank you for taking the time to read this book, and, in so doing, for being such a good advocate for the child with autism in your classroom.

REFERENCES

Ambitious About Autism (2017) *Obsessions and special interests.* Available from www.ambitiousaboutautism.org.uk/understanding-autism/behaviour/obsessions-and-special-interests (retrieved 13 October 2017).

Autism Key (2018) *What is Hyperlexia?* Available from www.autismkey.com/hyperlexia/ (retrieved 4 March 2018).

Canavan, C. (2016) *Supporting pupils on the autism spectrum in primary schools – A practical guide for teaching assistants.* Abingdon: Routledge.

Chia, N. K. H. and Kee, N. K. N. (2013) 'Effectiveness of Scaffolding Interrogatives Method: Teaching Reading Comprehension to Young Children with Hyperlexia in Singapore'. *Journal of the International Association of Special Education* 14(1) pp. 67–78.

Cosgrave, G. and McGuinness, L. (2011) *Sally Anne Test.* Available from www.educateautism.com/infographics/sally-anne-test.html (retrieved 1 July 2017).

Gray, C. (2018) *What is a social story?* Available from http://carolgraysocialstories.com/social-stories/what-is-it/ (retrieved 1 December 2017).

The National Autistic Society (2017) *Autistic pupils and transition.* Available from www.autism.org.uk/professionals/teachers/transition-tips.aspx (retrieved 1 October 2017).

The National Autistic Society (2017) *Communicating.* Available from www.autism.org.uk/about/communication/communicating.aspx (retrieved 4 July 2017).

The National Autistic Society (2017) *How do women and girls experience autism?* Available from www.autism.org.uk/about/what-is/gender/stories.aspx (retrieved 3 April 2018).

The National Autistic Society (2016) *Sensory differences.* Available from www.autism.org.uk/sensory (retrieved 10 April 2018).

The National Autistic Society (2017) *Social stories and comic strip conversations.* Available from www.autism.org.uk/16261 (retrieved on 04 April 2018.

The National Autistic Society (2016) *What is autism?* Available from www.autism.org.uk/about/what-is/asd.aspx (retrieved 13 October 2017).

Scottish Intercollegiate Guidelines Network (SIGN). *Autism – A booklet for parents, carers and families of children and young people with autism.* Edinburgh: SIGN; 2017 (SIGN publication no. ISBN 978 1 909103 46 7). Available from www.sign.ac.uk

Shelton, T.H. and Jalongo, M. R. (2016) *Practical strategies for supporting young learners with autism spectrum disorder.* Lewisville: Gryphon House Inc.

INDEX